T0328593

Cambridge Elements ≡

Elements in Generative Syntax
edited by
Robert Freidin
Princeton University

MERGE AND THE STRONG MINIMALIST THESIS

Noam Chomsky
University of Arizona

T. Daniel Seely
Eastern Michigan University

Robert C. Berwick
Massachusetts Institute of Technology

Sandiway Fong
University of Arizona

M. A. C. Huybregts
Utrecht University

Hisatsugu Kitahara
Keio University

Andrew McInnerney
University of Michigan

Yushi Sugimoto
University of Tokyo

CAMBRIDGE
UNIVERSITY PRESS

Shaftesbury Road, Cambridge CB2 8EA, United Kingdom

One Liberty Plaza, 20th Floor, New York, NY 10006, USA

477 Williamstown Road, Port Melbourne, VIC 3207, Australia

314–321, 3rd Floor, Plot 3, Splendor Forum, Jasola District Centre, New Delhi – 110025, India

103 Penang Road, #05–06/07, Visioncrest Commercial, Singapore 238467

Cambridge University Press is part of Cambridge University Press & Assessment, a department of the University of Cambridge.

We share the University's mission to contribute to society through the pursuit of education, learning and research at the highest international levels of excellence.

www.cambridge.org
Information on this title: www.cambridge.org/9781009462266

DOI: 10.1017/9781009343244

First published 2023

A catalogue record for this publication is available from the British Library

ISBN 978-1-009-46226-6 Hardback
ISBN 978-1-009-34326-8 Paperback
ISSN 2635-0726 (online)
ISSN 2635-0718 (print)

Merge and the Strong Minimalist Thesis

Elements in Generative Syntax

DOI: 10.1017/9781009343244
First published online: November 2023

Noam Chomsky
University of Arizona

T. Daniel Seely
Eastern Michigan University

Robert C. Berwick
Massachusetts Institute of Technology

Sandiway Fong
University of Arizona

M. A. C. Huybregts
Utrecht University

Hisatsugu Kitahara
Keio University

Andrew McInnerney
University of Michigan

Yushi Sugimoto
University of Tokyo

Author for correspondence: T. Daniel Seely, tseely@emich.edu

Abstract: The goal of this contribution to the Elements series is to closely examine Merge, its form, its function, and its central role in current linguistic theory. It explores what it does (and does not do), why it has the form it has, and its development over time. The basic idea behind Merge is quite simple. However, Merge interacts, in intricate ways, with other components including the language's interfaces, laws of nature, and certain language-specific conditions. Because of this, and because of its fundamental place in the human faculty of language, this Element's focus on Merge provides insights into the goals and development of Generative Grammar more generally, and its prospects for the future.

Keywords: Merge, minimalism, generative syntax, Strong Minimalist Thesis, third factor

ISBNs: 9781009462266 (HB), 9781009343268 (PB), 9781009343244 (OC)
ISSNs: 2635-0726 (online), 2635-0718 (print)

Contents

1 Introduction

A remarkable property of human knowledge of language is that it is infinite. You are not a simple recording device, capable only of repeating members of the finite set of sentences you have logged from experience. On the contrary, you can understand and produce *novel* utterances; in fact, the vast majority of all sentences that are understood and produced by humans across the globe are new. There are so many sentences, indeed an infinite number of new ones, that we all can, and should, use only our own. Although we all share the set of *words* we use, and it's perfectly ethical for you to use a thesaurus to find just the right word for the poem you're writing, the same is not true with sentences. There is no *sentence*-thesaurus; and taking someone else's sentence is very often not ethical – it's plagiarism. The infinity of sentences is the basis for this ethical principle; there are enough sentences to go around for each of us to use only our own. It's also the starting point of Generative Grammar, and of our discussion of Merge: a driving goal of the modern study of language is to determine and explain this property of discrete infinity.[1]

Your knowledge of language is *infinite*, but your memory is *finite*. Your knowledge of language therefore can't be just a list of memorized sentences. A central component of any theory of language, then, involves generating an infinity of sentences with finite resources. From a finite set of atomic elements, *lexical items* (roughly but not exactly words[2]) composed of irreducible linguistic features, the syntax must build an infinite array of hierarchically structured expressions interpretable at the 'meaning' interface and available for externalization at the 'form' (sound/sign[3]) interface, the so-called basic property of language (Berwick and Chomsky 2016).

---

[1] There's a one-word expression, a two-word expression, and so forth indefinitely, but no one-and -a-half word expression; that's "discrete" or "digital infinity." Among others, see Huybregts (2019).

[2] There is a significant difference between the abstract elements in the Lexicon, the "lexical items" that we refer to in the text, and a common sense notion of a *word* that may actually be spoken or written. We can leave this aside for present purposes.

[3] Despite historical prejudice, the sound modality is not critical to what makes *language* in the sense intended. The sign modality is equally relevant. Core, mind-internal aspects of language are shared across modalities (Lillo-Martin 1991; Emmorey 2002; Sandler and Lillo-Martin 2006, among others), and different language modalities seem to share modality-independent neural hardware; see Petitto (1987, 2005). For example, when sign-language users have damage in Broca's area (which is responsible for language production), they will show production errors, just as Broca's aphasia patients who use a spoken language could have a problem with language production. See Hickok and colleagues (1998) and Klima and colleagues (2002).

In current work the operation Merge[4] is the primary structure-building device of the syntax.[5] At the most general level, the picture looks like this. There is a lexicon consisting of a *finite* set of lexical items available for computation:

(1)   The Lexicon (storage bin for lexical material)

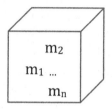

The Lexicon provides the raw material out of which Merge, the structure-building device, constructs larger objects. The Lexicon and Merge together constitute language in the narrow sense of the term.[6] We assume that lexical items are drawn as needed from the Lexicon and inscriptions of them are available for computation. Thus, a lexical item such as the noun *child* can be selected, and as many inscriptions of it as might be needed can be available, allowing such sentences as *One child slept while a second child played with another child*. Similarly, in mathematics there are multiple inscriptions of, say, the numeral three in an equation like $3x + 3y = 3$.

The computational process of structure building takes place within a Workspace (WS), which is updated in the course of the derivation of some expression. The WS is the set consisting of the material available for computation at a given derivational stage. Thus, the WS contains inscriptions of lexical items that have been entered into it and any objects constructed by Merge at earlier points:[7]

---

[4] Merge was first introduced in Chomsky (1994); see also Chomsky (2004a, 2013). For further discussion see Collins and Stabler (2016), Epstein and colleagues (2014, 2015), Epstein (2022), Collins (2017), among others. Section 7 provides a history of the development of Merge in the generative tradition.

[5] An even stronger view, to be reviewed in Section 8, is that Merge is the *only* operation of the syntax.

[6] See Hauser and colleagues (2002).

[7] We return in Section 3 to the technical specification of the WS, differentiating the set that is the WS from the sets that are syntactic objects within the WS; the WS is a set (that is a simple way to represent it) but the WS itself is not a syntactic object that is joined by Merge with any other object. See Collins and Stabler (2016); see also Kitahara and Seely (in press) and Marcolli and colleagues (in press) for a more complete formalization closer to the verson of Merge described here.

(2)   Preparing for an application of Merge

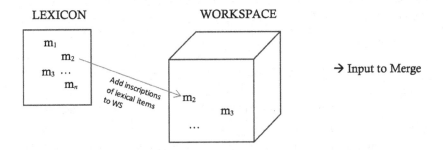

→ Input to Merge

Merge takes as input the WS, which contains computationally accessible material,[8] and it gives a modified WS as output. Informally speaking, Merge operates as follows:

(3)   Merge:
  (i)   'looks inside' the WS that it is applying to,
  (ii) targets material within the WS,
  (iii) builds from that targeted-material an object (i.e., it builds a nonatomic structure), which is now
  (iv) a new object within the WS, thereby modifying the WS.

To illustrate, suppose the WS consists of the lexical items shown in (4).

(4)   WS = [the, see, I, child]

Merge can take this WS as input and target the inscriptions of the lexical items *the* and *child* to create the set {the, child},[9] adding that set to the WS, and yielding (5).[10]

(5)   WS' = [see, I, {the, child}]

---

[8] As we'll see in more detail as we develop the framework, material that enters the WS is generally accessible for computation. However, in certain circumstances, material can be present in the WS but not accessible to Merge – this material is in effect 'hidden' from Merge. Generally speaking, an element is accessible unless rendered inaccessible in some way – we'll trace some of those ways in Section 6, and will consider various complexities associated with the notion 'accessibility.'

[9] The sets constructed by Merge correlate with the traditional construct 'phrase.' For ease of exposition, we will sometimes use both terms, set and phrase, designating the same object. We use standard curly brackets to indicate the sets/phrases constructed by Merge; to avoid confusion, we'll use square brackets, [], to designate the WS, which as pointed out earlier in this section is also a set, but not a syntactic object constructed by Merge.

[10] As we will see as we get into additional details, the inscriptions of *the* and *child* that were members of the WS do not themselves remain as members of the WS. The objects *the* and *child* are, in effect, replaced by the new set {the, child}, a result that will follow from independent third-factor principles, as will be clarified in Section 4.

Merge can then take this modified WS as input, target within it the object it just created, namely {the, child}, and join that object with *see* to produce the predicate phrase *see the child*,

(6)   WS" = [I, {see, {the, child}}]

and so on leading to the final abstract representation of the sentence *I see the child*.

As we'll see as we proceed, building our exposition through successive stages of complexity, Merge does not in practice freely target any element in the WS. In fact, there are very general principles, external and internal to language, that constrain just how Merge applies, with far-reaching empirical consequences. Note further that Merge is recursive in that it can target the objects that it creates in subsequent applications. In other words, in principle, the output of one application of Merge can serve as input to another application of Merge.[11]

Putting aside technical details, to be introduced in Section 6, this general picture provides a solution to the problem of discrete infinity. With a finite number of atoms and a finite number of computational mechanisms (so far, just one, Merge), the system has an infinite output; Merge can build a new syntactic object out of what it has already created. Merge, then, is *the* central component of language, where language is understood as a computational device generating linguistic objects receiving an interpretation at the meaning interface and a potential externalization at one of the SM interfaces (of sound or sign).

The goal of this contribution to the Elements series is to closely examine Merge, its form, its function, and its central role in current linguistic theory. We explore what it does (and does not do), why it has the form it has, and its development over time. The basic idea behind Merge is quite simple. However, Merge interacts, in intricate ways, with other components including the language's interfaces, laws of nature, and certain language-specific conditions. Because of this, and because of its fundamental place in the human faculty of language, this Element's focus on Merge provides insights into the goals and development of Generative Grammar more generally, and its prospects for the future.

To provide an outline of this Element: In Section 2, we review important background information, tracing the biolinguistic perspective on language assumed by Generative Grammar, that is, that language (in the narrow sense focused on here) involves a computational device embedded within an array of

---

[11] In a more general sense, what Merge builds within the WS at a given stage remains accessible for computation at later stages. Thus, if Merge puts X and Y together to form Z, then the new object Z is available for further computation.

human cognitive systems, and interacting with them. We also stress that a central goal from the generative perspective is to *explain* the properties of language, not merely to *describe* them. We then consider a number of key modes of explanation that have been pursued in the generative tradition, including recent work in minimalism, that seek to deduce seemingly complex properties of language from a few simple computational operations that interact with general laws of nature.

Having set the stage, we turn in Section 3 to Merge. The language faculty, by virtual conceptual necessity, involves a structure-building device. The goal is to stipulate as little as possible about it, deriving its seemingly complex properties from more general principles. We start with the simplest conception of Merge, that is, Merge as it would be in a 'vacuum' removed from other properties of language and from laws of nature – we start with Merge as a simple computational device. We then add in, step by step, different principles which affect Merge, and which thereby shape the form and function of this operation. Being a computational device, Merge conforms to general efficiency principles that all computation is subject to. But Merge is also a component of the human language capacity. Thus, Merge is subject to – and its operation is constrained by – general properties of human cognition, as well as language-specific principles. We trace such principles in Sections 4 and 5. Merge itself is maximally simple. But it interacts with general and language-specific principles in intricate ways, constraining its application; and these interactions conspire together to produce, ideally, just the empirical effects that we find.

Through Sections 2 to 5, we keep the discussion nontechnical: our goal is to present cutting-edge research on the nature of Merge in a fairly accessible way, minimizing formalism where possible. More formal details are presented in Section 6, which gives technical illustrations of the workings of Merge in key empirical domains; Section 6 is chiefly designed for those readers with a formal background in syntax. Many of the principles associated with Merge that are presented here represent very recent developments in the field; thus, we provide the historical context in Section 7, which reviews the development of Merge over time, tracing key historical antecedents, in an effort to provide the broader context for recent developments. We summarize and take up prospects for the future in Section 8. Overall, we hope that this Element's contribution will offer an introduction to Merge accessible to anyone generally interested in the study of language; but we also hope to provide some of the latest thinking on Merge that will be valuable to those with an extensive background in the field.

2 Background: Goals and Orientation of the Generative Enterprise

Merge is the central structure-building operation of language. To fully appreciate this, we need to understand how 'language' is understood, and trace a number of essential background assumptions, methodological considerations, and research goals.[12]

2.1 The Object of Inquiry: Language as Biology

Humans have an extraordinary capacity for language. As introduced in the mid-twentieth century, Generative Grammar is focused on this human capacity, seeking to determine its nature, to establish its core properties and, crucially, to *explain* those properties.

Since its inception,[13] the generative enterprise[14] has adopted the biolinguistic perspective on language, understanding language as a property of human biology, a cognitive faculty of the human mind. Language is a component of the brain in the same way that components of human vision, emotion, and other cognitive faculties are. Also crucial is the distinction between *possession* of knowledge of language and the *use* of that knowledge.[15] Consider the old Groucho Marx joke: *One day I shot an elephant in my pajamas. How he got into my pajamas I'll never know.* One's *knowledge* that there is an ambiguity here is quite different from one's *use of* that knowledge to amuse family members at the dinner table. Generative Grammar is concerned with the *knowledge* state, asking such questions as: What does knowledge of language consist of? What is the best theory of this knowledge? Where did it come from in the species? And, perhaps the most fundamental question of all might be put this way:

> How can there be just one human language and multiple languages at the same time?[16]

---

[12] The discussion in this section is meant to outline background assumptions essential to understanding the nature of Merge in current syntactic theory. For further detail, see, among others, Chomsky (1986, 2000, 2004b, 2017a, 2021b).

[13] Early works include Chomsky (1955, 1959, 1965, 1966a, 1968), and Lenneberg (1967), among others.

[14] As a historical note, the term 'generative enterprise' was first used in *The Generative Enterprise* (Chomsky 1982a; Chomsky 2004b).

[15] For a full account of the origins and break with structural linguistics, see Chomsky (1964). For further discussion, see Chomsky (1966b).

[16] For discussion, see Huybregts (2017). Given current genomic evidence, the evolution of Merge (or one Faculty of Language, FL) apparently antedates early human dispersals with subsequent distinct means of externalization (multiple languages). The idea that there is one human Faculty of Language, but multiple means of externalizing the products of that faculty resolves the paradox.

Take any typically developing human baby, place that baby in any linguistic environment, and the baby will, effortlessly for the most part, grow the ambient language – there's a massive naturalistic experiment on the planet right now that shows this. At a certain level of abstraction, then, there is just one human language faculty and thus one human capacity for language, which is, by definition, part of the innate biological endowment of *Homo sapiens* – your baby is born with it, your puppy is not. Yet, when we look around the world, we see literally thousands of mutually unintelligible languages, which are often characterized as radically different. How is this possible? What must the human language capacity be like for this to occur?

To understand how such questions are addressed, it's important to note that, from the biolinguistic perspective, language is understood as a computational system, one that builds structured objects from lexical material, where, in current theory, Merge is the structure-building device. This means, among other things, that Merge has the general properties of computational devices, and that language is subject to general principles of computational systems, something taken up in detail in later discussion.

It is important to note too that, in recent work in the generative enterprise, it is assumed that language is closely related to thought; a conception captured simply in William Dwight Whitney's phrase that language is "audible thought," a notion that revives a long tradition dating back thousands of years (Chomsky 2022a). Perhaps language is/constitutes thought (see Hinzen 2017, and Chomsky 2022a and Chomsky, in press). On this view, syntactic computation primarily serves the conceptual-intentional (CI) system. Externalization of language, through speech or sign, is secondary; in short, convergent syntactic computations necessarily receive an interpretation at CI but needn't be externalized (most language use is internal).

2.2 The Quest for Explanation

Humans are born not knowing any particular language, and grow to know one or more 'individual language(s),' like French, Ibibio, Russian, and thousands of others, in the course of typical development. Generative Grammar seeks to construct a theory of the cognitive system, the faculty of language, that underlies this process.

At one end of the process, we have the diversity of 'individual languages.' An individual language is taken to be a computational system that is a property of and internal to an individual (a biological property of humans). It is 'intensional' as well; a function in intension, the actual *grammar*, not its production nor just any grammar generating the same expressions. This notion of language is labeled *I-language*, essentially a lexicon and a computational system in the mind of a speaker.

Importantly, I-language is in sharp contrast with E-language, that is, externalization. The central concern of the computational system is the mapping from the Lexicon to the CI interface. I-language relies on structure, and structure only, ignoring linear order;[17] indeed, syntactic rules do not invoke linear order. Externalization linearizes structures in speech/sign. As a matter of principle, the objects constructed by Merge, namely sets, bars linear order from I-language. In contrast, sensorimotor mechanisms cannot see structure and are sensitive to linear order. The two are thus neatly separated and structure dependence is a necessary consequence, explained not stipulated. Structure dependence is nicely illustrated in acquisition. The child learning the language pays attention to what it never hears, namely structure, and not what is right in front of it, namely linear order. As shown by experiment, a thirty-month-old child[18] determines agreement in cases like

(7)   the boy and the girl are/*is in the room,

not by appeal to the simplest computational rule, adjacency. Rather, the child reflexively relies on something it never hears: the structure its mind creates. The child then assigns plurality by virtue of the nature of this abstract structure.

This crucial distinction between I-language and externalization is also highlighted by *homesign* or *emerging sign languages*. As Huybregts and colleagues (2016) discuss, homesign in deaf isolates or newly emerging sign languages (e.g., ABSL, Negev) in communities with a high incidence of congenital hearing loss amply demonstrate the profound distinction between possession of a language capacity and the use of that capacity. What's "invented" is *not I-language* itself (which develops naturally in the individual as determined by human genomics) but rather different ways of *externalizing* these in different communities.

As further illustration of this important distinction, Chomsky (2012, emphasis added) states:

> As discussed in Marr (1982), complex biological systems must be understood at different levels of analysis (computational, algorithmic, implementational). Here we discuss *internal language*, a system of knowledge, which we understand at a computational level. Since such a system is intensional, therefore not a process, there's no algorithm. In contrast, *externalization*, a process of using the internal system, may find an algorithmic characterization.

---

[17] For recent discussion see, among others, Chomsky (2021b).
[18] According to some experimental work, down to eighteen months (Shi et al. 2020).

Overall, the evidence is overwhelming that linear order is irrelevant to propositional structure and its interpretation.

I-languages represent the faculty of language in its *mature* state, attained after interaction with the environment (e.g., taking in linguistic input).[19] Babies are born with the faculty of language in its initial state.[20] A central goal is to understand how the innate computational system gives rise to I-languages. Crucially, what is the balance between the contribution of the language faculty (what the baby brings to the language-acquisition task), the contribution of the input, and the contribution of relevant general laws of nature? These conspire to explain how a child goes from having a general human language capacity to having a particular language, like Japanese.

It's clear from these central goals that the generative enterprise is concerned with explanation, not mere description. Though the resulting empirical findings are crucial to the enterprise, it is not enough to describe the properties of some language, using whatever unconstrained mechanisms might be available to get the job done. The goal is not to use any type of mechanism that can cover the data. Generative Grammar has, from the outset, been concerned with the explanation of the properties of human language – not with just *what* the properties are, but *why* those properties take the shape that they do, *why* they are this way and not another, and *why* they might exist in the first place.[21] Ideally, analysis of the data contributes to a (conceptually plausible and empirically motivated) account of the central question traced above: How can there be one language and multiple languages at the same time?

Explanation is difficult. How do we know when we've explained something? One aspect of explanation involves simplicity. Historically, what we find throughout the development of the generative enterprise is a reduction of the inventory of theoretical postulates within the syntax. What was language-particular (e.g., the rules of French), construction-specific (e.g., the rules of relative clause formation), and syntax-specific (as opposed to a more general rule or principle, not unique to syntax) in earlier stages of the framework was reduced, or factored down, or eliminated, distilling out more general principles – standard practice in science generally. The effects of these postulates were (in large part) derived from the interaction of the syntax (which will be characterized in more detail as we proceed) with the systems that it necessarily interfaces

---

[19] For important discussion, dealing with certain confusions regarding the notion 'linguistic input,' see Epstein (2016).

[20] The theory of this initial state is often labeled Universal Grammar, *UG*, adapting a traditional notion to a new context.

[21] This fundamental point is missed in the state-of-the-art language models (e.g., GPT3, see, for example https://garymarcus.substack.com/p/noam-chomsky-and-gpt-3). For important discussion see Chomsky (2022b). See also Chomsky and Moro (2022).

with, systems of sound/sign (sensorimotor) and thought (conceptual intentional). And the effects of these language- and construction-specific postulates were derived from general principles of computational systems; notions of computational efficiency, such as 'least effort,' ideally laws of nature.[22]

A good starting point for explanation, then, is the recognition that three factors enter into the growth of language in the individual (as briefly alluded to earlier in this section; see Chomsky 2005). First is the innate biological endowment, the human faculty of language. Second is experience, interaction with the environment. Third are laws of nature not specific to language, including considerations of computational efficiency, something natural for a computational system like language:[23]

(8)   First factor: genetic endowment
         Second factor: experience
         Third factor: laws of nature

From the outset, the goals regarding the empirical content of the innate computational system, the first factor, were in conflict. On the one hand, descriptive adequacy (i.e., getting the facts right) seemed to require that the innate endowment be rich in available mechanisms, initially including multiple and rather complex subcomponents for structure building and structure manipulation (see Section 7 for further details in a historical context). It seemed that the innate system had to be quite complex if the facts of language were to be accounted for – even a superficial look shows that language is complex, diverse, mutable. On the other hand, given the apparently recent evolution of language in the species, the innate computational system must be simple – a complex, multifaceted system could not have evolved in so short a time. Explanatory adequacy (i.e., accounting for the acquisition of language) required uniformity, simplicity, and an account of the ease and rapidity of language acquisition. Furthermore, the quest for simplicity is a defining feature of theory building. As Einstein notes: "The grand aim of all science is to cover the greatest possible number of empirical facts by logical deduction from the smallest possible number of hypotheses or axioms" (Einstein 1954, p. 282).

The attempt to deal with these conflicting demands, that the innate computational system account for complex facts and yet be simple, characterizes much of the history of the generative enterprise. How can the system be made as simple as possible while at the same time maintaining descriptive adequacy?

---

[22] See Section 7 for more detailed discussion of the history of the development of Merge and the changes that have occurred in the components of the syntax.

[23] As noted earlier, language is a cognitive faculty, understood as a computational device.

Needless to say, this is a challenging task, and marks a central research goal of the framework.

We've taken steps toward explanation when we've developed the simplest system that meets certain conditions. One is the condition of *learnability*: the theory must account for how a child can, through the interaction of the innate language faculty and the environment, grow an I-language (recalling our discussion of 'I-language' in subsection 2.2). A second condition is *evolvability*: the innate computational system must have emerged in accord with the conditions on the evolution of *Homo sapiens*.[24] As noted in Chomsky (2021b, p. 8):

> With regard to evolvability, genetic studies have shown that humans began to separate not long after their appearance.[25] There are no known differences in Language Faculty, narrowing the window for its emergence. Furthermore, there is no meaningful evidence of symbolic behavior prior to emergence of Homo Sapiens. These facts suggest that language emerged pretty much along with modern humans, an instant in evolutionary time. If so, we would expect that the basic structure of language should be quite simple, the result of some relatively small rewiring of the brain that took place once and has not changed in the brief period since.

The competing requirements of these first two conditions on explanation are set in clear relief: to account for the rapidity and uniformity of acquisition, the innate computational system would seem to need to be complex;[26] recent evolution demands the opposite.

A final condition is that the innate system must accommodate all possible languages while barring all impossible ones. A series of studies designed by Andrea Moro, for example, shows that language areas of the brain react normally when a subject is presented with invented languages that model actual languages. However, this is not the case with invented languages that are not like actual ones; in this case, the subject's brain activity is that of puzzle solving, not language-area activation. Indeed, in acquisition, children ignore what is seemingly most accessible to them, namely, linear order, and appeal instead to the nonlinear structures created by the mind (i.e., created by Merge), Moro (2016); see also Chomsky and Moro (2022).

---

[24] See Berwick and Chomsky (2016). See Huybregts (2017), and see footnote 14 in subsection 2.1.

[25] See Ragsdale and colleagues 2023 for recent evidence that this demographic picture might be less tree-like, with a more subtle pattern of weak admixture and divergence occurring prior to 120,000 to 130,000 years ago.

[26] In fact, through much of the history of the development of the theory, UG *was* quite complex, consisting of a variety of disparate mechanisms and language-specific principles.

Overall, a genuine explanation is achieved only if it keeps to mechanisms that satisfy the conditions of learnability, evolvability, and universality. As traced earlier in this section, these conditions are at odds, or at least have been in earlier stages in the development of the theory.

A guiding principle in this quest for explanation is the Strong Minimalist Thesis (SMT). Over the years, SMT has taken a number of forms,[27] but in the present context we understand it in two ways. First, conformity to SMT requires that the structures of I-language are generated by the simplest operations. Hence, Merge must take the simplest possible form, and the number of additional structure-building operations should be minimized (ideally, entirely eliminated). As much as possible, then, the form and the function of necessary operations like Merge are reduced to third-factor principles such as computational efficiency, understood in this context as natural law.[28] The innate system should be reduced to a minimum, and appeal to the third factor should be concomitantly maximized. Second, SMT can also be understood as the thesis that the Faculty of Language (FL) is an 'optimal' solution to certain language-specific conditions (LSCs, see Section 5 for more details). In this case, the content of SMT will depend on the LSCs. In the best of all worlds, these conceptions will converge: The simplest theory of the initial state optimally satisfies LSCs.

2.3 The General Picture

Let's display the general picture that has emerged over the years. First, there are assumed to be irreducible lexical features of 'form' (i.e., sound/ sign) and meaning that are combined to comprise the atoms of syntax, abstract lexical items, inscriptions of which are entered into the WS. The structure-building operation Merge constructs syntactic objects from lexical material and from the syntactic objects it has already constructed, yielding hierarchically structured objects that are then available to the interface systems, the sensorimotor (SM) for the externalization of 'form' in speaking, signing, and writing, and the conceptual-intentional (CI) involving 'thought' for planning and other such cognitive activities. We stress that the CI interface is primary (as we'll see in more detail as we proceed); SM is secondary:

---

[27] For important relevant discussion of SMT, see Chomsky (2000b, 2004a) and also Freidin (2021).

[28] For example, see D'Arcy Thompson's work (Thompson 1917). See also Turing (1952).

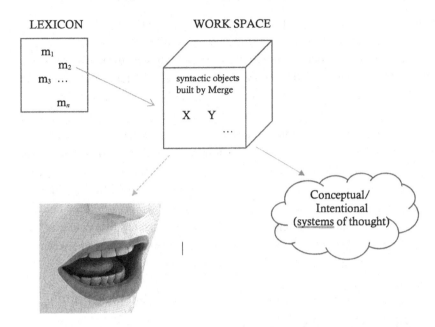

Given SMT, a central goal is to minimize structure-building operations by making the single indispensable structure-building operation, namely, Merge, as simple as possible. To do this, there is an intricate balance in the requirements of the interfaces and in the role of third-factor considerations, that is, laws of nature, and language-specific properties. To the extent that we can account for properties of language by appealing to these basic factors, we have reached explanation, something we hope to illustrate in greater detail as we proceed.

3 The Form of Merge

Having traced the bigger picture of the nature of the inquiry, let's turn attention to Merge itself, laying out in this section its basic characterization. The goal is to understand some of the details of the structure of the operation, and its function as a computational device. We first consider Merge in its unconstrained form, the form it takes outside of any first or third-factor principles; it's the form Merge would take in a 'vacuum,' removed from the principles of computation, the laws of nature, and language-specific conditions that restrict its operation. In line with SMT and evolvability, this basic form of Merge is maximally simple, and it is important to see this up front. In short, we don't want to build into the formal definition of Merge what follows from a more general principle. Merge interacts with various principles in such a way that Merge might seem compli-cated, but this is something of an illusion. We seek to *stipulate* as little as possible regarding Merge, deducing as many of its properties as we can from more general laws. There are many examples of a mechanism being influenced by forces external to it: thus, in mitosis, the resulting cells are spherical not because of biology but because of physics, similarly with the hexagonal structure of honeycombs. And there are many examples of natural systems that are effectively maximally simple but this simplicity is masked by constraints imposed by laws of nature so that 'on the surface' their behavior seems to require complex description. Perhaps the most famous example concerns the motion of the planets when viewed against the apparently fixed background of stars. As is familiar to astronomers, this planetary motion can be accurately described by a complex set of forty to sixty partial circles of different diameters superimposed on each other, called "epicycles." However, all this complexity can be eliminated by a single natural constraint, namely, Newton's law of gravitational force declining inversely as the square of distance between the sun and the planets, as outlined by Kepler and Newton.

3.1 Unconstrained Merge: Merge in Its Simplest Form

Merge can be characterized as in (9):

(9)　　　Merge (WS) → WS'

In its unconstrained, most general form, Merge is a maximally simple structure-building, relation-creating operation. It takes a Workspace (WS) as input; it combines elements in the WS; and it returns a modified WS as output, where the WS represents available computational resources. Merge applies to the WS and, informally speaking:

> it targets elements, $P_1, \ldots P_m$, within WS,
> it puts the targeted-elements into a set, $\{P_1, \ldots, P_m\}$ (expressing that the elements are in a relation with each other by virtue of being members of the same set, traditionally a 'phrase'), and
> the newly created set is now a member of the WS, defining a new state of the WS, which is then available for further computation.

In somewhat more formal terms, the initial definition[29] of Merge is:

(10)　　　$\text{Merge}(P_1, \ldots, P_m, WS) = WS' = [\{P_1, \ldots, P_m\}, \ldots]$

Merge takes as input the WS including the elements, P_1 through P_m, that are selected from the WS, and it gives the output WS', of which the set $\{P_1, \ldots, P_m\}$ is a member, where '...' represents everything in the WS minus $P_1, \ldots, P_m$.

---

[29] Note that the most fundamental operation is essentially Form Set; that is, put any number of objects into a set, adding that set to the WS. What is referred to as 'Merge' is, in effect, Form Set restricted to two; thus, Merge is binary set formation. We discuss below why Merge is binary.

Merge thereby constructs the familiar objects of syntax, like noun phrases and predicate phrases. To put, say, *the* and *man* into the set {the, man} is a simple way to express that the words are now part of a larger object, a phrase, traditionally referred to as a noun phrase.[30] A set is a simple and readily available notation to express the core idea of a phrase.[31] In this way, syntactic structure is built.

As formulated, Merge is simple. A host of questions immediately arise:

How are $P_1 \ldots P_m$ selected?
How many elements are selected, and why?
Do the targets of Merge, $P_1 \ldots P_m$, remain in the WS when they are put into a set; if so, why/why not?
What happens to other material in the WS not directly affected by Merge?

We will address these and other questions step by step, as we proceed. Our immediate goal is simply to present Merge in its simplest and unconstrained form.

Our next task is to show that the way Merge applies in language is constrained by forces external to it, specifically by third-factor considerations of computational efficiency and by language-specific constraints. What Merge can (and cannot) apply to within the WS and what it yields is in large part determined by the fact that Merge is a component of a computational system operating within the human organism. We first outline third-factor considerations that constrain how Merge applies (Section 3 and 4); we then turn to certain crucial language-specific constraints (Section 5).

3.2 On (Identical) Inscriptions with Merge and Other Formal Systems

An important preliminary point has to do with what Merge operates on within the WS that it takes as input. We said in Section 1 that the Lexicon contains lexical items and that lexical items can be drawn out of the Lexicon and entered into the WS. This is obviously metaphorical – a lexical item is not literally removed from the Lexicon when it enters the WS. Indeed, a single lexical item can be entered into the WS multiple times as in our earlier example *One child slept while a second child played with another child*. What's entered into the WS, then, is an *inscription* of the lexical item (while the 'original' lexical item remains in the Lexicon, available for further selection). Technically, Merge

---

[30] This structure is, in turn, crucial to interpretation at the interfaces.

[31] In Section 7, we outline the development of generative grammar's evolving views on human phrase structure, ultimately leading to the Merge Operation, including discussion of how the label of a phrase is determined.

targets inscriptions in the WS; thus, it targets the inscription of *child* and the inscription {*one, child*} in the course of the derivation associated with the sentence above.

Language, like any other formal computational system, is about manipulation of the inscriptions that serve as its atomic units. And parallel to other formal systems, there are structurally identical inscriptions. Thus in the formula [*p* & ~*p*] in logic there are structurally identical inscriptions, multiple instances, of *p* in this case, and these instances are interpreted in the same way. There are a number of ways for structurally identical inscriptions to arise in language as well. The WS for our simple example contained three separate inscriptions of *child* (i.e., *child* was entered into the WS from the Lexicon three times)[32]. Language has another way for an inscription to arise in the WS: Inscriptions arise as a result of an application of Merge, as we'll see in subsection 3.4. What we stress from the outset, since it plays a critical role in later discussion, is that language has a unique property, distinguishing it from other formal systems: *Only language has structurally identical inscriptions that are not invariably interpreted in the same way.* Thus, in the sentence *Many people praised many people*, the identical inscriptions of the phrase *many people* are interpreted differently – clearly the two instances of *many people* can refer to different groups.[33] All of this will become clearer as we proceed; our immediate goal is to stress a feature of Merge: it is operating on inscriptions within the WS, just like any other computational system.

So far, we've introduced the basic, unconstrained form of Merge – Merge in a 'vacuum,' as it were; that is, the unconstrained form of Merge, without consideration of extrinsic factors that affect its application. We then put in place preliminary points on the inscriptions that arise in the course of structure building. Let's turn next to external forces that Merge interacts with, which constrain the application of Merge and that result in intricate empirical effects.

3.3 Constrained Merge: Merge as a Computational Device and a Component of an Organic System

Merge is a computational device, one that is a component of an organic system, and thus is constrained in its application by restrictions imposed by organic systems and by general principles governing the operation of any computational mechanism; it is, in short, necessarily subject to the third factor, as described in

---

[32] As we'll see in more detail as we proceed, we distinguish the identity relation (the very same inscription) from distinct inscriptions that are identical (they have the same form) but are, under specific conditions, (i) interpreted in the same way versus (ii) not interpreted in the same way.

[33] Thus, the logical form is roughly: For many x, x people, there are many y, y people, such that x chased y, and not: For many x, x people, x chased x.

subsection 2.2. Third-factor principles are not necessarily known in advance. Various principles have been and are being explored, and new ones will undoubtedly be discovered as research progresses. In the following section, we present one line of inquiry.

3.3.1 Merge is Binary: The Most Economical Form of Merge Targets Two and Only Two Objects

We start by noting a general property of computation: it is Markovian. At each step in a derivation, a computational system operates on a certain representation; it does not have the capacity to access earlier steps of computation.[34] In the case of Merge, this means that Merge has access to the WS only at a fixed derivational moment (namely, access to WS at the stage where Merge applies); it has no 'memory' of what the WS looked like at earlier stages. The question of this subsection is: at the stage in the derivation where Merge applies, how many objects within the WS does Merge operate on, and why? The simplest form of structure building, with Merge characterized as just 'form set,' could operate on any number of WS objects.[35] But there are external forces that constrain selection of input objects.

One third-factor principle associated with computation involves a form of simplicity: less computation is simpler than more. Of course this is not unique to linguistics; it's a scientific truism representing the basic methodology of science. Simplicity-by-least-effort expresses itself in various ways. One involves the number of elements in the WS that Merge can target. The simplest choice for natural language syntax is two elements at a time because syntax involves relations between distinct objects. To build any relevant syntactic structure at all, Merge must target a minimum of *two* objects. By parsimony, then, the simplest form of Merge is binary; Merge targets two and only two elements of the WS on any given application.[36] Two is necessary; by parsimony, we seek a system where two is sufficient.

---

[34] This is taken for granted in formal systems (in a 'vacuum') but has no effects since everything is carried over; in a proof, you can go back to an earlier line, which, in the relevant sense, is still in the WS. It becomes significant for Merge because of third-factor considerations constraining the WS, as we'll see.

[35] This allows Form Set to operate on just a single object. As the simplest illustration, suppose the Lexicon contains just one element, a, and Form Set creates a set. Then, it could create the set $\{a\}$, and then $\{\{a\}\}$, and $\{\{\{a\}\}\}$, and so on ad infinitum, effectively yielding the successor function. The form of Merge that we investigate later in this section is binary (putting *two* objects into a set), the minimum necessary for natural language syntax. As we'll see in more detail, language-specific conditions, more precisely Theta Theory, require more than one target of Merge for language.

[36] On the economy-based argument for the binarity of Merge, see Collins (1997).

We won't go into details here, but there is established, wide-ranging empirical evidence that the phrases of language are binary.[37] As a simple kind of example, consider:

(11)   Q: Which house is yours?
         A: It's the third yellow house.

The noun phrase with an ordinal number and an adjective, as in *the third yellow house* above, is not adequately represented by the nonbinary set {the, third, yellow, house}. This would allow the meaning that it's the third house and it is yellow since both the modifiers *yellow* and *third* are in the same minimal phrase as the noun *house* and so should be able to independently modify that noun. What it actually means is: it's the third house out of the yellow houses (thus, 'it's the third yellow house but not the third house overall' is not a contradiction). We can account for this under binary phrases. If only two objects are assembled at a time, we can build the larger noun phrase in binary chunks: first, {yellow, house}, where *yellow* modifies *house*; then {third, {yellow, house}}, where *third* modifies the complex object {yellow, house}; then {the, {third, {yellow, house}}}. Under the binary structure, *third* is not directly paired with *house* and hence we correctly disallow the unavailable interpretation that it is the third house (which happens to also have the property that it is yellow). Details aside, our immediate point is that the empirical evidence for binary phrases is well established.

This shapes the definition of Merge as follows:

(12)   Merge(P, Q, WS) = WS' = ({P, Q}, X_1, . . ., X_n) = Binary Merge

Merge takes a WS as input; it targets two (and only two) terms P, Q within that WS; it puts P, Q into the set {P, Q}, thereby adding the newly created set to the WS and yielding a new derivational stage, WS'. The key point here is: the binary property of Merge does not have to be *stipulated* for Merge, but rather it follows from a general notion of simplicity.

Besides how many objects Merge targets (just two), a related question has to do with *what* Merge targets: are *any* two inscriptions in the WS available to Merge, and what, at an even more basic level, is meant by an object being 'in' the WS?

3.3.2 Merge Is Subject to Minimal Search: External and Internal Merge

For an operation to apply to objects, it must first locate those objects. Let's abstract out the 'locating' operation, formulating and exploring its properties – referring to the operation as Search. Search locates the (two) items in the WS

---

[37] See, for example, the classic work of Kayne (1981, 1983, 1984, 1994); for important discussion, see also Collins (1997, 2022).

that (binary) Merge applies to – in a stepwise fashion. We expect Search to conform to third-factor requirements for Minimal Computation. Therefore, what in the WS is available to Merge is naturally limited by minimal (least effort) Search.

With this in mind, consider (13), the output of (an earlier application of) Merge, which constructed the object {b, c}.

(13)   WS = [a, {b, c}]

The WS defines the set of objects which could in principle be accessed by Search (and hence available to Merge).[38] Of the resources in the WS, what does Search locate, and why? Note, for example, that the elements *b* and *c* are not *members* of the WS (in purely set-theoretic terms). Does this affect how they are (or are not) located?

To better explore these questions we need some terminology. In order to distinguish 'a (set-theoretic) member of the WS' from a more general notion of 'in the WS,' we adopt the notion 'term of,' defined as follows:[39]

(14)   X is a *term of* Y iff X is either (i) a member of Y or (ii) a member of a term of Y.

The elements *a* and *{b, c}* are members of the WS (13) and are thus also terms of that WS. The objects *b* and *c*, on the other hand, are *terms* of the WS, not *members* of it. Let's adopt 'term of' in order to have a vocabulary to more fully detail the concept of Minimal Search.[40]

Search operates in a stepwise fashion: it first locates some P (from the WS), and in a second step locates some Q to merge with P. Applied to the WS in (13), that is, [a, {b, c}], Merge will first locate P, where P can be any *member* of [a, {b, c}], so either *a* or *{b, c}*. Members of the WS are all equally available with *Least Search*; the members are the first objects found looking into the WS and the first Search step can take any one of the members. The terms *b* and *c* in (13) are not members of that WS and hence are not candidates for (first-step) Search. Staying for now at an informal, intuitive level, locating *b* or *c* takes more computation (a more extended Search) than locating the containing set

---

[38] We'll see later that some objects are rendered inaccessible to computation if certain conditions hold, something we can put aside for right now.

[39] See Chomsky (in press) and Chomsky (2021b). See also the 'contains' relation of Collins and Stabler (2016, p. 46).

[40] For pioneering discussion of the formal nature of the Search procedure of syntax and its consequences for syntactic theory, see Ke (2019). Ke points out that (i) the search target T and search domain D depend on the operation O that Search is feeding. If O is Agree, then T is a particular feature (depending on the probe), and D is the c-command domain of the probe. If O is Labeling, then T is any feature, and D is the object being labeled. Ke (2022) discusses examples of 'least effort/Minimal Search' in other domains, including visual search and computer science.

{b, c}; simply put: it's easier to take one step than two; locating a term within a member of WS is a two-step process involving locating that member and then locating a term in it, and thus takes more computation than locating that member or any other member of the WS. It follows that the first step (locating P) in any application of Search will take any member (and only a member) of the WS as (the Merge target) P – this is least effort.

What about the second step of Search, locating Q (to merge with P)? In the second step there are two options. One is that once Search locates P, it looks inside P for Q. A second option is for Search to locate Q in the same way as it located P; that is, it takes the WS as the Search domain and by Least Search can take any member of that WS as Q.[41] Overall, this gives us two general modes of application of Merge, what are referred to as *External Merge* (EM) and *Internal Merge* (IM). With EM the two Merge targets P, Q are separate members of the WS. With IM, Q is contained within P.

Over-simplifying for purposes of illustration, consider the key points in the derivation of a simple passive sentence like *The apple was eaten.* Assume that inscriptions of the relevant lexical items have been entered into the WS, and that *the* and *apple* are merged to form {the, apple}. We would then have the WS:

(15)   WS = [eaten, {the, apple}]

Suppose the first step of Search locates the transitive verb *eat(en)* (= P) and then in the second step locates the noun phrase {the, apple} (= Q). Both steps conform to Least Search since the targeted objects are both members of the WS. With the objects now located we apply Merge, using those objects:

(16)   Merge(*eaten,* {the, apple}, WS) where P = *eaten*
                                             Q = {the, apple}

Since Merge creates within the WS the set {P, Q}, the output of this application of Merge would be:

(17)   WS' = [{eaten, {the, apple}}][42]

---

[41] In the first step of Search, any member of the WS can be selected. In the second step, it's the first relevant object, where 'relevant' is determined by various factors. Our discussion here is focused mainly on Merge applying to NP arguments; hence 'NP' is relevant, as we'll see in the example later in this section.

[42] It should be asked: why isn't the output

   [eaten, {the, apple}, {eaten, {the, apple}}]

where P (= *eaten*) and Q (= {the, apple}) remain as members of the WS. We return to exactly this question in subsection 3.3.3.

This is referred to as *External Merge* (EM): merging P, Q where both P, Q are members of the WS, that is, neither P nor Q is contained within (is a term of) the other.[43] The pairing of *eaten* and {the, apple} is crucial for interpretation: since the verb and the noun phrase are within the same minimal phrase (the set {eaten, {the, apple}}), the noun phrase is interpreted at the CI interface as the semantic object of the verb (thus, it means 'ate the apple').[44] Suppose we now enter into the WS (an inscription of) the passive auxiliary verb *was* and then (externally) Merge it with {eaten, {the, apple}}, yielding:

(18)   WS = [{was, {eaten, {the, apple}}}]

This yields the passive predicate, which we'll refer to as the verb phrase (VP).

Suppose Search applies to the WS (18) and in the first Search step locates the VP, a member of the WS; thus P = VP. As we pointed out above, the second step of Search can look inside P and, in this case, find within it the NP {the, apple} as Q.[45] Thus,

(19)   Merge(P, Q, WS), where P = {was, {eaten, {the, apple}}}
        Q = {the, apple}

The output of this application of Merge, referred to as Internal Merge, is:

(20)   WS' = [{{the, apple}, {was, {eaten, {the, apple}}}}]

With EM, P and Q are separate; with IM, Q is contained within P.[46] There is a single operation, Merge, with two modes of application.

Notice further that Internal Merge necessarily results in structurally identical inscriptions of P, which in this case is {the, apple}. Given its formulation, Merge combines its targets P and Q in a set; it doesn't alter their structure.[47] This is a property of all derivations in any formal system. In the present case, it means

---

[43] Note that the earlier construction of {the, apple} is also an instance of EM.

[44] Chomsky (in press) proposes that EM always creates such semantic relations, referred to as Theta Structures; that is, that EM (and only EM) builds the propositional domain. We return to this idea and to some of its consequences in Section 5.

[45] As stated earlier in this section, our focus here is on IM of arguments; hence, we assume that Merge is searching for an NP; then, the NP {the, apple} is in fact the first NP found looking into the VP; this is least search – it is the fewest search steps to find an NP.

[46] Internal and External Merge, as traced earlier in this section, are the *only permissible* applications of Merge under the assumptions developed here. See Epstein and colleagues (2012) for some relevant discussion. Importantly, while prior work has sometimes framed EM as Merge of separate objects (see e.g., Chomsky 2004a: 110), EM here refers specifically to Merge of two members of the WS. Other forms of Merge have been proposed, including what is referred to as Parallel Merge (Citko 2005) and Late Merge (Lebeaux 1988); but we argue later in this section that these are extensions of Merge, rather than subcases of Merge.

[47] In previous literature this is referred to as the No-Tampering Condition: the targets of Merge remain intact (Chomsky 2007). The No-Tampering Condition follows directly from the formulation of Merge (Freidin 2021).

that identical inscriptions of {the, apple} arise: {the, apple} is a term of P = {was, {eaten, {the, apple}}}, and {the, apple} *is* Q, and both P and Q must be intact. The output is necessarily (20) with identical inscriptions of {the, apple}. The output can't be, for example:

(21)   WS' = [{the, apple}, {was, {eaten}}]

where P (somehow) changes from {was, {eaten, {the, apple}}} to {was, {eaten}}. Indeed, altering P in this way would destroy the semantic relation between the transitive verb and its semantic object; but, crucially, it would simply not be an instance of Merge (as Merge has been defined) since it would be replacing P with an entirely new P'. We stress that this is a general property of all computation.

3.3.3 Preservation

The application of Merge is restricted by the third factor, entailing that Merge is binary and its two targets are located by Minimal Search, allowing only Internal and External Merge. In this subsection we make explicit another important property of computation, Preservation: the interpretation of an inscription does not change in the course of computation.

Preservation is a general constraint, normal for all computation in formal systems. There can be no valid computation unless each inscription is interpreted in one and only one way. Since language is a computational system, we expect Preservation to hold. It certainly does for material that is not directly affected by Merge. All nontargets of Merge in the input WS remain in the output, WS'. To somehow remove such objects is an extreme form of change of interpretation; thus, deletion of an inscription from the WS is disallowed.

Preservation is not a syntactic operation and is thus not subject to the Markovian property of such operations. Rather, Preservation by its very nature must be able to 'scan' each derivational step to be sure that an inscription has not changed interpretation. Thus, Preservation can detect the *identity* of inscriptions. To illustrate, consider again the instance of IM involved in the passive. The input and output WS are repeated here, where our focus is just on the object {the, apple}:

(22)
$$\text{WS} = [\{\text{was}, \{\text{eaten}, \{\text{the, apple}\}\}\}]$$

$$\text{WS'} = [\{\{\text{the, apple}\}, \{\text{was}, \{\text{eaten}, \{\text{the, apple}\}\}\}\}]$$

Preservation can see both the input (WS) to and the output (WS') of IM, and thus can see that {the, apple} is the very same inscription in the input/output, as indicated by the dotted line between the derivational stages. Thus, {the, apple} in WS is {the, apple} in WS'; it's one and the same inscription. That is the identity relation.[48] Likewise with the passive VP {was, {eaten, {the, apple}}}; it's the same inscription in WS and WS'. That is how Preservation must work. It tracks the same inscription, ensuring that the inscription does not change its interpretation. The *operations* of the syntax, however, are Markovian. Thus, the identity information encoded with the dotted line is lost for the operation Merge. All Merge sees is WS', and looking *only* at WS', it sees two distinct inscriptions of {the, apple} that happen to be structurally identical (i.e., that have identical form). In short, with respect to {the, apple} in the case above, Preservation sees the very same inscription. Merge, and other operations of the syntax, sees two inscriptions that are structurally identical; that is, that have the same form, with the same lexical items hierarchically arranged in the same way. Syntactic operations have no information about how these inscriptions were created.

3.4 Identical Inscriptions: Repetitions and the Copy Relation

As we noted in the previous section, in formal systems, identical inscriptions have the same interpretation. If q occurs on multiple lines of a proof, the structurally identical q inscriptions are interpreted in exactly the same way; likewise in the equation 3+3=5, the structurally identical inscriptions of '3' have the same interpretation – we can't take the second instance of '3' to mean 2 and conclude that the equation is true.[49] The standard assumption with formal systems, then, is *Uniform Interpretation of Identical Inscriptions* (UIII): structurally identical inscriptions are interpreted in exactly the same way. This is not to be confused with Preservation: from Preservation it follows that a single inscription can't change its interpretation in the course of the derivation. From UIII, on the other hand, it follows that for formal systems any set of structurally identical inscriptions in a given 'Workspace' are interpreted in the same way.

But, as we noted in subsection 3.2, human language is different. Structurally identical inscriptions can have distinct interpretations, as in *Many people praised many people,* where there are different groups of people. So, with

---

[48] The strict identity relation X=Y ('the same inscription') can only be determined across derivational steps. So, when we say 'identical inscriptions' or 'structurally identical inscriptions' we mean two inscriptions that have identical form.

[49] As stated in Chomsky (2021b, p. 17, fn 25); "The issue has arisen in the history of mathematics in a debate over validity of Newton's proofs, at a time when there was no clearly formulated theory of limits. Was there equivocation in his use of zero and 'as small as possible'"? See Kitcher (1973). For an alternative view and further discussion of the copy-repetition distinction, see Freidin (2016).

language, the question arises: When are identical inscriptions interpreted in the same way and are therefore *copies*,[50] and when are identical inscriptions *not* interpreted in the same way and are therefore *repetitions*? The distinction is illustrated with the following simplified, abstract representations.

(23)   {{many, people}, {praised, {many, people}}}
             = the syntactic representation that at SM yields *Many people praised many people.*

(24)   {{many, people}, {were praised {many, people}}}
             = the syntactic representation that at SM yields *Many people were praised.*

In (23) the identical inscriptions of {many, people} are repetitions, hence not interpreted in the same way, as noted previously.[51] In the passive (24), where identical inscriptions necessarily arise, they are copies and interpreted in exactly the same way; (24) clearly does not have an interpretation where there are distinct groups of people. On an intuitive level, with (23) there are two separate noun phrases that happen to constitute structurally identical inscriptions, each noun phrase having its own interpretation, while in (24) there is one noun phrase that is 'in two positions simultaneously.' How is this difference captured in formal terms under our given assumptions so far?

With formal systems, there is an implicit operation, *Form Copy* (FC),[52] which assures the same interpretation of identical inscriptions; that is, FC applies to all structurally identical inscriptions in a formal proof, assigning them the same interpretation. But, plainly, the application of FC is restricted in language; it does not freely apply to any and all identical inscriptions. For language, we can define it as:

(25)   Where X, Y are structurally identical, FC(X, Y) interprets X, Y as copies, that
             is, the inscriptions are interpreted in exactly the same way

The default is that identical inscriptions are repetitions, becoming copies only if assigned to the copy relation via FC; it's just that FC is restricted in language.

To illustrate how FC applies, consider again the (most directly relevant) derivational steps of the simple passive sentence *Many people were praised.*

---

[50] 'Copy' and 'repetitions' are standardly used terms from the literature. See Chomsky (2019a, 2019b, 2021b).

[51] Of course, it's possible for repetitions to be interpreted as co-referential. Thus, in *He thinks he's smart*, the identical inscriptions of *he* are repetitions, but can still have the same referent.

[52] FC does not create structure; rather it is interpretive, assigning the copy relation to structurally identical inscriptions under certain conditions.

Assume that lexical material is introduced into the WS and multiple instances of EM have applied, building up to the passive verb phrase:

(26)   WS = [{were, {praised, {many, people}}}]

Next, IM applies, as we've seen:

(27)   Merge(P, Q, WS), where P = {were, {praised, {many, people}}}   = application of IM
                                   Q = {many, people)

yielding the output:

(28)   WS' = [{{many, people}, {were, {praised, {many, people}}}}]   = output of IM

Here is a critical point: as noted above, operations of the syntax are Markovian, as is true of computation generally. Merge and FC have access to <u>only</u> the current state of the WS, prohibiting any 'look back' at earlier derivational points. The syntax sees the WS at the stage represented by (28), not (26) nor anything earlier. The syntax has no way to 'see' into the derivational past to determine whether a single noun phrase has been 'moving around' within the syntactic structure, or whether there are two separately constructed noun phrases that happen to constitute identical inscriptions.

Let's assume that we are at the point in the derivation where interpretation is going to take place,[53] that the syntactic object within the current WS, represented by (28), is 'opened up' to interpretation by the interfaces. It is at this point that FC applies since the copy relation is relevant to the semantics; for example, FC contributes crucial information for the semantic interpretation of inscriptions. It is an operation that applies to a syntactic object, and which provides 'instructions' to the interfaces relevant to interpretation just at the point that the object is entering semantic interpretation; FC provides the information 'these two identical inscriptions are copies' and the semantics thus knows to interpret them in the same way. Suppose FC applies to the WS in (28) and, given the Markovian property, all it sees is (28). FC applies, thus: FC({many, people},

---

[53] In technical terms, the point at which FC applies is referred to as the *phase level*. It goes beyond our immediate concerns to go into further detail; it suffices to note that the pieces of structure built by Merge are organized into chunks called 'phases' corresponding to the clausal and verbal domains. The key idea is that Merge builds to a phase, the phase is opened up to interpretation by the interfaces, and then Merge continues building to the next phase, and so on. This phase-based, cyclic computation instantiates third-factor simplicity in that it reduces computation: the system doesn't build an object only to retrace its steps and modify that same object later. Relevant consequences of this phase-based approach are explored in Section 6. Technically, the phases are CP and *v**P – see Section 6. Nothing really hinges on the construct 'phase' until we get to more complex cases; see Section 6 for further comment; but we do want to acknowledge at this point the phase-based approach that is assumed throughout.

{many, people}), and the copy relation between the two structurally identical inscriptions is thereby established.

As noted above, the information provided by an application of FC is critically important to CI (interpret structurally identical inscriptions X, Y in exactly the same way). It is also relevant to SM. SM uses the 'copy relation' information supplied by FC as an instruction to not pronounce the lower copy, which we indicate in gray below:

(29)   WS' = [{{many, people}, {were, {praised, {many, people}}}}]

An efficiency consideration at SM is to pronounce just one (the highest) of a set of copies. Thus, the pronunciation is *Many people were praised*.

With the basic workings of FC in place, let's consider next the second of the pair we discussed earlier in this section, repeated here as (30):

(30)   {{many, people}, {praised, {many, people}}}

In this structure, FC must be blocked; if FC applies, then the two identical inscriptions of {many, people} are interpreted in the same way, a problematic result. Note, for example, that if FC were to successfully apply in (30), we would expect the lower copy to delete (i.e., not be pronounced) at SM; that is, we expect the structure to surface with the pronunciation *Many people praised*. But this is the wrong result. Why does FC apply in (29), but is blocked in (30)? More generally, what are the restrictions (and why) on the application of FC? We answer this question in subsection 5.2 (see also subsection 6.1.2), arguing that FC is blocked in (30) since there are multiple theta roles from the same verb (both the 'praise-er' and the 'praise-ee' roles) associated with *many people*. But, for now, further details regarding how FC works need to be developed.

Since FC applies to terms of the WS, it follows that it, like Merge, must *locate* its targets within the WS. This is done by computationally optimal Search. While Merge builds syntactic structure, FC aids interpretation of those structures by establishing relations between elements within them. Thus, FC will apply to two structurally identical inscriptions, X, Y, only if they are found by Minimal Search. The smallest set in which the copy relation can hold between X and Y is {X, Z} where Y is a term of Z. Therefore X, as a sister of Z, *constituent-commands* (abbreviated *c-commands*) Z and any element contained in Z, and thus X c-commands Y.[54] In this way, Minimal Search for FC requires that X and Y are in a c-command configuration (henceforth *cc-configuration*). In

---

[54] There are three fundamental relations that result from Merge. Relative to elements X, Y; (i) X, Y can be co-members of a set; (ii) Y can be a term of X; and (iii) Y can be a term of the co-member of X, which is c-command. Thus, we appeal to the simplest relations.

accord with SMT, relation-creating operations like FC will keep to cc-configurations. This has important consequences for when copies can arise, which we'll explore in some detail later in the Element (see Sections 5, 6). The central goal for now is to introduce the motivation for, and basic form of, the copy-relation-creating device Form Copy of natural language.

In this section we first considered Merge in its most basic form; the minimal specification of Merge for language is that it targets (two) elements within the WS and creates a new object from these elements; Merge is a simple structure-building device: it builds a piece of structure out of material within the WS, thereby adding that newly created structure to the WS. That's it. But the application of Merge is shaped by nonlinguistic-specific constraints. Merge applies with Minimal Computation and, thus, it is binary and locates objects through Minimal Search. Furthermore, Merge is constrained by general principles of computation, specifically, Preservation. These external forces conspire to constrain the application of Merge. When we factor in these external principles, Merge takes the following form:

(31)   Merge(P, Q, WS) = WS' = [{P, Q}, . . .]

Summarizing the results so far, Merge is binary. Only External and Internal Merge are possible, and are optimal given Minimal Search. Merge minimally modifies the WS, by Preservation. Merge yields identical inscriptions, which may be assigned the copy relation by FC.

4 Merge and the Non-expansion of the WS: Restricting Resources/Minimal Yield

Before considering further properties of FC and its interaction with Merge, we consider in this brief section an issue that has been implicit in the discussion of Merge so far and that is important to make explicit, and to clarify.

Third-factor-compliant Merge minimally modifies the WS that serves as its input: Merge does not alter the material already in the WS, meaning that the elements not directly affected by Merge remain; and the targets of Merge are not themselves altered. But what happens to targets of Merge with respect to their status as members of the WS? External Merge as we have formulated it in the preceding discussion may be more formally represented as:

(32)   WS = [a, b, c]
         Merge(a, b, WS)
         WS' = [{a, b}, c]

But there's a question: Why aren't the targets of Merge, *a*, *b*, included as members of the output WS'; why isn't the output:

(33)   WS' = [a, b, {a, b}, c]

Shouldn't Merge *minimally* disrupt the WS, adding {P, Q}, but leaving the WS *completely* undisturbed otherwise, such that every member of the input WS is also a member of the output WS'? If not, what's happening to P, Q?

In constructing formulas of propositional calculus, all propositions introduced remain fully available to further manipulation; with a proof of formal logic: if *p* is in line one of a proof and is joined with *q*, which is on another line of the proof, via the rule of addition, the inscription *p* in line one remains, and an identical inscription occurs in the conclusion [p & q]. All else equal, the computation of language should be no different. The seemingly simplest statement of (third-factor-compliant) Merge is: Merge(P, Q) results in identical inscriptions of P, Q remaining in the WS; that is, the output (33).

As stressed above, Merge is a component of the human linguistic system and is, naturally, constrained by the relevant properties of that system. One constraint, following the work of Sandiway Fong, is that the computational system seeks to minimize resources.[55] As Fong notes: "The device we call the brain is a marvelous organ, endowing us with the capacity for symbolic thought, language and reasoning far beyond what other animals have exhibited."

But, Fong continues:

> this marvel is not the computational powerhouse that we might assume. The biological unit of computation, the neuron, possesses a slow communication mechanism, a signal requires around a millisecond to cross the chemical synaptic gap, and after certain electrical pulse trains, a synapse might require up to 140-150 ms to recover (Testa-Silva et al. 2014). Although (much faster) direct electrical synapses exist in our nervous system, e.g. they can be found in the retina, slow chemical synapses predominate in the human brain. There is also evidence that the brain does not maximize sensory capacity, which suggests the computational brain is the weak link (or bottleneck) in the chain from external stimulus to thought (and response). For example, we know our eyes are capable of both incredible sensitivity, i.e. single photon level (Tinsley et al. 2016), and resolution, achieving peak acuity of 77 cycles/ degree (Curcio et al. 1990), all unnecessary for scene analysis. Even an eagle only possesses eyesight about 3 times better than humans, yet arguably, the eagle requires far better resolution. Human olfactory thresholds can be of the order of parts per billion (ppb) (Wackermannová et al. 2016). Our eardrums

---

[55] See Fong (2021) and Chomsky (2019b), for further details. As discussed there, the same problems bar all extensions of Merge: Parallel Merge, Sidewards Merge, Late Merge (which also violates SMT for independent reasons); such extensions expand the WS.

can detect vibrations smaller than the diameter of a hydrogen atom (Fletcher & Munson 1933). In case after case, the brain does not make use of the full resolution of available sensory inputs. Perhaps the answer is that it cannot, as a slow organic system, it does not possess the necessary bandwidth, and therefore, it must (selectively) throw away much of the signal. The idea that this pressure for efficiency also pertains to both data and computation in language, born out of biological limitations, was termed *The Third Factor* by Chomsky (2005). (Fong 2021, p. 3)

There is a general principle, Resource Restriction (RR),[56] holding of and encoded in the human brain. An instantiation of RR holding of language, which we refer to as *Minimal Yield* (MY), guarantees that Merge yields the fewest possible new terms that are accessible to further operations, thereby limiting subsequent Search. Merge(P, Q, WS) necessarily constructs one such accessible term: {P, Q} itself. By MY, it should yield no more than that. Since Merge is the sole combinatorial operation of human language, it must meet conditions imposed by organic systems and hence is restricted in its output by MY.[57]

Minimal Yield answers the question about what is 'left behind' from Merge. To exemplify, consider again the following derivation:

(34)   WS = [a, b, c]

       Merge(b, c, WS)   P = b; Q = c

If the targets of Merge remain as members of the WS, the result would be:

(35)   WS' = [a, b, c, {b, c}]

But output (35) violates MY: the number of accessible terms in the output WS has increased by more than one. Not only is the new object {b, c} accessible, but, recalling our earlier discussion, there are now also two distinct inscriptions *b* and two distinct inscriptions *c*. Another, somewhat more intuitive way to think about it is this. Merge targets *b* and *c* and puts them into the set {b, c} – the inscriptions *b*, *c* in {b, c} are the original inscriptions from the input WS. Thus, the inscriptions *b* and *c* that are *members* of the output WS (35) are *new* elements, new inscriptions, and hence new terms. So Merge is resulting in

---

[56] This principle is arguably not unique to syntax, but more general, potentially relevant for the acquisition of phonology by 'forgetting' unused options (see, for example, Mehler and Dupoux 1994), and see Charles Yang's work on probability distribution of grammars in acquisition (Yang 2002, 2004).

[57] Defined in this way, MY diverges from the earlier principle 'Restrict Computational Resources' of Chomsky (2019a) and the similar 'No proliferation of roots condition' of De Vries (2009). These prior conditions limited cardinality of the WS (or 'number of roots' in De Vries's terms). Instead, MY limits *accessibility of terms*, which subsumes cardinality.

more than one new term in the output in violation of MY. In order to satisfy MY, the output WS would have to be:

(36)   WS' = [a, {b, c}]

where only one new term, {b, c}, arises. MY determines the fate of these 'excess' inscriptions.

5 Language-Specific Conditions on the Computational System for Human Language

Merge builds structures used by the interfaces CI and SM. Of the two interfaces, Merge primarily serves CI, constructing a language of thought, and thus it will be constrained by the requirements of CI, considered to be language-specific conditions on interpretation. The computational system (i.e., language in the narrow sense) has to satisfy conditions specific to the organic system of humans. One important condition has to do with Theta Theory (TT): language must provide *predicate/argument structure* at CI;[58] that is, it provides the structures with respect to which certain kinds of semantic information can be determined. This section briefly reviews TT as a language-specific condition (LSC) and explores how it affects application of Merge.

So far, we've seen that Merge in its most basic form is a simple structure-building operation; it creates a piece of structure from material in the WS, adding that structure to the WS. We then explored certain third-factor principles that Merge is necessarily subject to, particularly principles related to computational efficiency. For example, the third-factor-compliant form of Merge is binary and subject to efficient Search. Critically, Merge is also subject to the first factor; that is, to language-specific conditions like TT. Theta Theory is not a general efficiency condition constraining formal systems; it is unique (as far as we know) to language. It's important, then, to consider the consequences of the interaction of Merge with such conditions, as it accounts for certain unique properties of language compared to other formal systems.

5.1 Theta Theory

Theta Theory is a theory of thematic relations between predicates and their arguments. Thus, the predicate *chase* has two arguments, *x chase y*, each of which is associated with a *theta role* (in this case: Agent-of-CHASE, intuitively

---

[58] Predicate/argument structure is the representation of lexical structure, including the theta-role assigners (predicates) and theta-role assignees (arguments), in the format of set theory. Thus, as mentioned in the text, a theta role assigner like a transitive verb (say, *chase*) is combined with an argument (like *the cat*) in the set {chase, {the, cat}} to create the configuration for the 'chase-ee' theta role to be assigned to {the, cat}, yielding the relevant semantic interpretation.

the 'chaser' and Patient-of CHASE, the 'chase-ee'). In its classic form,[59] TT requires an isomorphism between theta roles and arguments: every theta role must be assigned to one, but only one argument; and every argument must receive one, but only one theta role. It captures the fact that gratuitous arguments unconnected to the meaning of a sentence yield gibberish, as in (37)

(37)   *Juan sleeps the building Tom.

where the noun phrase arguments *the building* and *Tom* have no relation to the rest of the sentence – they do not receive a theta role. Likewise, we don't get (38)

(38)   *Juan put

where the theta roles of the verb *put*, informally 'the-thing-put' and 'location,' are unassigned. Additionally, a single argument can't be assigned multiple theta roles; thus (39)

(39)   *The dog saw

can't mean that the dog saw itself (where *the dog* is assigned both the 'see-er' and see-ee' theta roles).

Interpretation is computed from the meaning of lexical and phrasal items and the structural relationships between those items. Structure building, and hence the structure building operation Merge, will be constrained by the (language-specific) requirements of interpretation, including TT.[60] Just what are the consequences of the interaction of Merge with TT? Just how is Merge constrained by this language-specific condition?

5.2 Duality of Semantics: EM for Theta Positions, IM for Non-Theta Positions

'Duality of Semantics' refers to an interpretive distinction between what is produced by EM and what is produced by IM. As Chomsky (2008, p. 140) notes:

> At the semantic interface, the two types of Merge correlate well with the duality of semantics that has been studied within generative grammar for almost forty years, at first in terms of "deep and surface structure interpretation" (and of course with much earlier roots). To a large extent, EM yields generalized argument structure (θ-roles, the "cartographic" hierarchies, and

---

[59] See Chomsky (1981) and references therein for further discussion.

[60] As we've noted, Merge itself does not know what will be the interpretation of an object it builds. However, the interpretative component can act as a 'filter' on the output of Merge, and hence constrain its operation.

similar properties); and IM yields discourse-related properties such as old information and specificity, along with scopal effects. The correlation is reasonably close, and perhaps would be found to be perfect if we understood enough – an important research topic.

More recently Chomsky (2020, p. 44) states:

> If you look quite generally at the interpretation of expressions, it falls into two categories. There is one category which yields argument structure (theta roles and the interpretation of complements of functional elements). There is another category which is involved in displacement, which has kind of discourse-oriented or information-related properties or scopal properties and so on, but not argument properties. That's duality of semantics. If you think about it a little further, you see that the first type, argument structure, is invariably given by external MERGE. The second type, non-argument structure (other factors) is always given by internal MERGE.

Let's consider how this distinction arises in the current system. The hierarchical position of an argument relative to a predicate (i.e., a theta role assigner) determines the assignment of theta roles and therefore the interpretation of an argument. For example, the argument NP *the dog* merged with a transitive verb (like *chase*) forms the {V, NP} configuration associated with the theta role of Patient (chase-ee).[61] The primary theta position is direct object (object of a transitive verb, or object of an adjective, preposition, or nominal), and this position can be created only by EM, not IM. Consider a verb and its object. If the WS is

(40)   WS = [V, NP, ...]

then since neither V nor NP is a term of the other, only EM, that is, Merge(V, NP, WS), is possible. Thus,

(41)   EM and only EM creates object position, the primary theta position.

The other major theta position is predicate-internal subject (i.e., the external argument position). For the moment, let's put aside technical details (see Section 6 for formal discussion) and illustrate with the simplified structure in (42).

(42)   {Bill, {chased, dogs}}

Assume that *chased* assigns a theta role to the NP argument *Bill*. In (42), *Bill* must have been externally merged into this position; that is, we build the

---

[61] As in, among many others, Williams (1994), Harley (1995), Hale and Keyser (2002). A relatively recent alternative view takes the Patient theta role to be assigned in a Spec-Head relation with a dedicated functional head, analogous to assignment of Agent to the specifier of v^* (or Voice in work following Kratzer 1996). See, for example, Borer (2003) and Lohndal (2014).

predicate {chased, dogs} and then combine the subject with this predicate using EM. This external argument could never be filled by IM. Suppose, for instance, that *Bill* starts in the object position

(43)   {chased, Bill}

and then is internally merged to form the subject position:

(44)   {Bill, {chased, Bill}}

This violates Preservation. The single inscription *Bill* is interpreted in more than one way: by virtue of its initial position, and by virtue of the position into which it merges by IM. Hence, such an application of IM is disallowed.

What we find, then, is EM (and only EM) creates the primary theta positions. Suppose we strengthen this to a segregation of EM and IM, yielding the principle of Duality of Semantics:[62]

(45)   *Duality of Semantics*: EM, and only EM, creates theta positions.

That is, only EM creates a theta position, IM creates non-theta positions. Duality is, in large part, a consequence of the interaction of Merge, Preservation, and TT. Thus, EM of an argument (NP, PP, . . .) always creates a theta position. If an argument were to be externally merged to form a non-theta position and stays there, TT is violated (the argument won't be assigned a theta role). If an argument were to be externally merged to form a non-theta position and subsequently internally merged to form a theta position, then Preservation is violated (its interpretation would change)[63]. On the other hand, IM never creates a theta position; any argument internally merged to form a theta position will necessarily change its interpretation, in violation of Preservation. Thus, Duality follows.

Note further that Duality as in (45) is an economy condition that sharply reduces options for application of Merge: merger of an argument that creates a theta position is necessarily via EM; and IM of an NP argument always creates a non-theta position. Thus, IM and EM are segregated, contributing to the overriding meta-condition of Resource Restriction (RR) in a natural way; in short, choice points are reduced.

Duality has a number of important consequences. Consider, for instance, the classic distinction between (46) and (47), recalling our earlier notation where a strikethrough indicates that the element is present in the syntactic object (for CI interpretation), but not pronounced at the SM interface.

---

[62] See Chomsky (2019b).

[63] However, IM from a theta to a non-theta position is clearly allowed; this is natural since the target NP is not adding to its already-established interpretation.

(46)   *the man chased ~~the man~~

(47)   the man was chased ~~the man~~

For (46), suppose that an instance of the NP argument *the man* is externally merged into the (semantic) subject position.[64] Then, following FC(the man, the man), a TT violation will result: a single theta role assigner, *chased*, is assigning more than one theta role to the same element – where the 'same element' is structurally identical inscriptions of a copy pair formed by FC. If we try to internally merge *the man* from object to subject position, we violate Duality (IM is not to a theta position) and Preservation. (46) is thus correctly disallowed. (47), on the other hand, is perfectly fine: by Duality, we can't externally merge (an instance of) *the man* into subject position since the subject of the passive is a non-theta position. However, we can in this case internally merge *the man* from object to (non-theta) subject position, running afoul of neither TT/Duality nor Preservation. See Section 6 for full details.

The modes of application of Merge, the conditions Merge is subject to, and the nature of FC together give us just the right empirical results for standard cases, as illustrated in this section (see also Section 6 for detailed illustrations). But, SMT, as conceived here, also has an important *enabling function*, predicting the existence of phenomena that are otherwise completely unexplained. One of these is obligatory control.

5.3 The Enabling Function of SMT: Deriving Obligatory Control

Recall from subsection 2.2 that SMT is understood in two ways. It's the thesis (i) that the structures of I-language are generated by the simplest operations, ideally just Merge and (ii) that the language faculty is an 'optimal' solution to certain language-specific conditions, including TT. We now turn to a further consequence of adherence to SMT.

In earlier stages of the development of Generative Grammar, control phenomena, as in (48)

(48)   The man tried to read a book.

led to the development of an entire subcomponent of the grammar with a designated empty NP type,[65] namely PRO, and principles of construal such

---

[64] That is, suppose *the, man* are selected and then Merged into {the, man}, which is Merged to form {chased, {the, man}}. Then, *the* and *man* are selected from the Lexicon a second time and entered into the WS. Merge then builds a separate instance of {the, man} and merges it to {chased, {the, man}}. In this case, two distinct instances of {the, man}, each built separately, would be EM'ed into their respective positions.

[65] See, for instance, Chomsky (1981) for analysis within the Government and Binding Framework. See also Landau (2013) and Reed (2014).

that (48) was interpreted as: the man x, x tried x to read a book. Under current assumptions, none of this is required. Rather, the central properties of the 'control component' simply fall out as a consequence of SMT; nothing beyond what we've proposed is necessary.

Let's consider (48), avoiding full technical details for right now (see Section 6). The argument NP *the man* can be merged into the lower (theta-) subject position:

(49)   {{the, man}, {read, {a, book}}}

We then build up to

(50)   {tried, {to, {{the, man}, {read, {a, book}}}}}

By Duality, {the, man} cannot be internally merged into the higher subject position; that higher (predicate-internal) position is a theta position of the predicate *try* and hence internally merging it would run afoul of Duality. But nothing prohibits externally merging an identical inscription of {the, man} (built separately from the first one) into the higher subject position.[66] Thus, the WS would contain the already-constructed object, {tried {to, {{the, man}, {read, {a, book}}}}}. Then, *the* and *man* are selected from the Lexicon, entered into the WS where a new object {the, man} is created. This new object, {the, man}, is then externally merged with the predicate to give:

(51)   {{the, man}, {tried {to, {{the, man}, {read, {a, book}}}}}}

Duality is satisfied (EM is always to a theta position) and TT is satisfied; in this case, unlike in *the man chased the man* reviewed in subsection 5.2, there are two distinct theta role assigners associated with the inscriptions of *the man*, namely, *read a book* and *tried*. Thus, Merge can generate the representation (51) – as long as identical inscriptions of *the man* are each externally merged into their respective positions. Now FC can apply to the representation (51), with no knowledge of how (51) was constructed. The conditions for FC(*the man, the man*) to apply are met – it is in fact a cc-configuration, and thus *the man, the man* are assigned to the copy relation, the lower copy is unpronounced (as a consequence of the economy condition discussed above), and (51) *the man tried to read a book* meaning *the man x, x tried to x read a book* results. Exactly the right result with significant empirical advantages, as we'll see in Section 6.

As mentioned in subsection 2.2, one way to understand the *Strong Minimalist Thesis* (SMT) is as a thesis about the nature of language, that is, about FL: the thesis that FL is an optimal solution to certain language-specific conditions

---

[66] Note that there is some similarity to the older Equi-NP Deletion analysis of Rosenbaum (1967).

(LSCs), the topic of UG. Theta Theory, including Duality of Semantics, is an LSC and thus shapes the operation of the computational system. Duality of Semantics (like RR) constrains how Merge applies, thereby contributing to the reduction of computational complexity. Also, if FC applies in accord with TT, then FC is further restricted.[67]

If this picture is tenable, then LSCs such as TT (including Duality) and properties rooted in the human brain such as RR are design specifications for I-language, with significant empirical consequences.

6 Illustrations

Up to this point, (i) the form and function of Merge have been outlined, (ii) key third-factor (computational efficiency) and first-factor (language-specific) principles have been traced, and (iii) the consequences of the interaction of Merge with these principles have been explored. Merge, and the way that it can (and can't) operate, is reasonably clear. In this section, we turn to a somewhat more technical exploration of Merge, working our way through a set of central derivation types. In Sections 1–5, we have tried to keep the discussion at a fairly nontechnical level, focusing on key concepts and components rather than formal technicalia. The more formal implementation of the framework is ultimately important, however, and so in this section we consider technical details, presupposing familiarity with recent work.

6.1 The Central Cases

6.1.1 A Simple Sentence with a Transitive Verb

To get started, let's work our way through a (seemingly) simple sentence like

(52)   The fox ate a pear.

We assume, first, that inscriptions of relevant lexical material are inserted into the Workspace (WS) as needed.[68] Given this, the direct object *a pear* can be

---

[67] Under current assumptions, Duality constrains Merge, which builds structures, but not FC, which assigns the copy relation, while such structures with copy relations are interpreted in accordance with univocality. Both Duality and Univocality are rooted in TT, but the former is construed as a condition on Merge, whereas the latter is how structures (built by Merge and assigned copy relations by FC) get interpreted.

[68] We leave open the nature of lexical insertion; the assumption is simply that lexical material can be retrieved from the Lexicon and entered into the WS at any point in the derivation – nothing in the subsequent discussion hinges on how this is done. One option is insertion of lexical items via an operation 'Select' (Collins and Stabler 2016). Alternatively, lexical items might simply be freely accessible.

derived via the mapping shown below, where lexical items *a* and *pear* are members of the input WS:[69]

(53)   (input) WS = [*a, pear*]

MERGE(*a, pear*, WS) =

(54)   (output) WS' = [{*a, pear*}]

Now consider the construction of the predicate phrase, technically a $v*P$[70] phase, from this point. The NP *a pear*, constructed as in (53)/(54), is available for further computation.[71] We can now (externally) merge the Root R EAT with the NP (assuming R has been inserted from the Lexicon into the WS):

(55)   WS = [R, NP] where NP = {*a, pear*}

Merge(R, NP, WS) =

(56)   WS' = [{R, NP}]   = EM of argument to create a theta position

It is not clear to us at this point whether object shift, whereby the NP complement of R is raised to create a specifier position of R, is optional or obligatory,[72] but we assume it occurs. Such raising of the object must be by IM given Preservation (the specifier of R[73] is a non-theta position). If we were to create a duplicate instance of the object, *a pear,* and try to EM it into the Spec-of-R

---

[69] Technically, Merge maps WS directly to WS'. Despite this, we could *informally* describe the internal workings of the process like this: Constrained by efficient Search, Merge looks into the WS (53) and finds the two WS members *a* and *pear* (both locatable by Search). Merge creates the set {*a, pear*} and adds this to the output WS'. In a vacuum, the inscriptions *a* and *pear* would appear twice, as in (i).

(i)   WS' = [*a, pear,* {*a, pear*}]

However, Merge obeys Minimal Yield (MY), which would be violated in the mapping from (53) to (i) in that the WS would be expanding beyond just one. Thus, MY requires that the inscriptions *a* and *pear* each appear only once in the output WS' (54). One could thus informally think of (i) as an intermediate step between (53) and (54), though it is important to note that (i) is never computed given the formal apparatus developed above.

[70] We assume the labeling algorithm of Chomsky (2013, 2015), and assume that proper labeling occurs at relevant points; that is, at the phase level – we leave the details of labeling aside given our focus here on Merge itself.

[71] Note that the derivation of (52) is built through successive applications of Merge, specifically External Merge. Note further that Duality of Semantics does not play a role in these applications of Merge; Duality is relevant only when the merger of arguments (NP and embedded CP) is involved, where it requires EM of an argument to saturate a theta position; as we've seen, IM cannot be used to fill a theta position.

[72] See Lasnik (2022) for extensive discussion; see also Johnson (1991), Lasnik and Saito (1991), Koizumi (1993, 1995), and Lasnik (2002).

[73] We use the traditional expressions 'Spec-of-X' and 'Complement-of-X' for expository convenience; these terms (Chomsky 1970), and the notions of subject or object that they represent (Chomsky 1965, p. 71) were never introduced as syntactic primitives. By 'Complement-of-R'

position (and then relate the structurally identical inscriptions of *a pear*, one in Spec-R and one as object of R, by FC), Duality would be violated – EM of an argument must be to a theta position – thus, EM is simply not available in this instance.[74] If the object raises to Spec-R, meaning IM has applied, identical inscriptions of the object will automatically be produced. The original position of the object as complement of R must remain given Preservation. Thus, we get:

(57) $WS = [\{\{a, pear\}, \{R, \{a, pear\}\}\}] = [\{IA, \{R, IA\}\}]$, IA is the internal argument[75]

Least Search finds only the higher of the identical inscriptions and hence (as we saw in Section 3), Minimal Yield is not violated with this instance of IM. Such 'object shift' occurs with Exceptional Case Marking,[76] something we'll turn to a bit later.

We then merge in the phase head v^*, and externally merge the external argument (EA) *the fox*, which would have been constructed in parallel, to yield

(58) $[\{EA, \{v^*, \{IA, \{R, IA\}\}\}\}]$ EA = {the, fox}

We are now at the v^*P phase level where Form Copy (FC) can apply. Relevant here would be FC(IA, IA), assigning the copy relation to the structurally identical inscriptions of the IA, {a, pear}. The phase-head complement, RP={IA, {R, IA}}, is accessed by the interfaces and, given the Phase Impenetrability Condition (PIC),[77] is inaccessible to Merge from here on – an expression of the bottom-up, cyclic nature of the syntax. What this means for interpretation at the SM interface, if externalization is activated, is that only the higher copy will be pronounced, yielding the linear effect of object shift. Note further that we assume the labeling system of Chomsky (2013, 2015); and, specifically, that the phase-head complement is labeled by the 'shared prominent feature' option of the labeling algorithm; that is, in {IA, {R, IA}} = {{the, fox}, {R, {the, fox}}}, Search finds the phi features inherently borne by the lexical iterm *fox* and those phi features of R, and assuming these features match, the object is labeled by the

we simply mean the co-set-member of R. 'Spec-of-R' would be the co-set-member of {R, IA}, and so on.

[74] A question arises regarding how expletives enter into the derivation. Expletive *there*, for instance, is not an argument but must be externally merged into a non-theta position. We leave this matter aside.

[75] The external/internal distinction refers to older analyses where an argument that is interpreted as the subject of a predicate is syntactically external to that predicate, as opposed to an object of a predicate, which would be internal to the predicate. We use the terms here to distinguish the two arguments in v*P, for expository convenience.

[76] We presuppose familiarity with ECM and related conceptual/empirical issues discussed in the literature.

[77] We assume that CP and v*P are the phases. In Chomsky (2015), feature inheritance was assumed, along with the 'phase head' property. We put aside that complexity here.

phi features themselves. In short, a single unique feature set (the phi features shared by IA and R) serve as the label.[78]

Let's continue the derivation up to the next phase, the C phase. First, we merge INFL (I).

(59)   WS = [{I, {EA, {v*, {IA, {R, IA}}}}}]

Note that the grey shading indicates material that is no longer accessible to Merge given the PIC.

The EA *the fox* now merges (for labeling purposes) to Spec of INFL (the syntactic subject position). This must be by IM; the Spec-of-INFL position is a non-theta position, and hence, by Preservation, merging an NP argument to this non-theta position can't be by EM. That is, we can't build a duplicate of *the fox*, EM this duplicate in the Spec-of-INFL position, and then, at the phase level, use FC to make the identical inscriptions of *the fox* copies. Thus, EA will internally merge to Spec of INFL:[79]

(60)   WS = [{EA, {I, {EA, {v*, {IA, {R, IA}}}}}}]

As traced in Section 4, this application of Merge does not violate MY; the lower instance of EA, *the fox*, is not found by Search, only the higher identical inscription of the EA is; thus, the lower instance is inaccessible to Merge (hence the strikethrough of the lower inscription) and so does not count as expanding the WS. We then merge the phase head C, reaching the next phase level, CP

(61)   WS = [{C {EA, {I, {EA, {v*, {IA, {R, IA}}}}}}}]

Now that we are at the phase level, FC(EA, EA) can apply, rendering copies. Assuming that labeling is appropriately carried out, the derivation is complete, ultimately yielding the structure pronounced as *the fox ate a pear*.

It's worth pausing for a moment to consider a few points from this simple derivation. We stress first that there is just a single operation, Merge. The expressions 'internal' and 'external' Merge are for ease of exposition and have no theoretical significance; they are simply modes of application of Merge. Merge is doing the same thing with both 'external' and 'internal' Merge. Merge is always (i) targeting elements P, Q, and (ii) adding the set {P,

---

[78] The full details of the labeling mechanism go beyond the scope of the present discussion; see Epstein and colleagues (2014).

[79] Note, furthermore, that efficiency considerations also favor IM over EM, where possible. On the one hand, IM requires one instance of Merge; EM, on the other hand, as specified in the text, requires building a separate instance of {the, fox} and then externally merging it to create the Spec-of-INFL position.

Q} to the WS. Given third-factor principles, an identical inscription remains only in the case of IM.

It is worth repeating also that the unmarked case for identical inscriptions is that they are interpreted as distinct; identical inscriptions will be copies only if they are rendered so by Form Copy – and this only happens in the c-command configuration at the phase level, as noted in Section 3. Thus, with (61), it is at the phase level that the result of FC(EA, EA) will be available to the interface where that information is used to interpret the inscriptions in the same way. If FC has not presented this information to the interfaces, then identical inscriptions are not interpreted in the same way.

6.1.2 Active versus Passive

Consider next the cases in (62) and (63):

(62)   The fox was chased (by someone)

(63)   *The fox chased   = meaning 'the fox x, x chased x'

Sentence (62) is perfectly acceptable, but not (63) on the interpretation "the fox chased itself." Let's work through the derivations under current assumptions. We first Merge the object and the verbal root R (i.e., CHASE):

(64)   WS = [{R, IA}] where internal argument (IA) = {the, fox}

Whether or not the object shifts to Spec-R, there is no way to construct a licit derivation from (64) to the surface form (63). Let's merge in the phase head v^*,

(65)   WS = [{v^*, {(IA), {R, IA}}}] where IA = {the, fox}

At this point, an object must be merged in Spec-v^* to discharge v^*'s Agent theta role. Given Preservation, we can't achieve this via IM of IA (either from Complement-R or, with object shift, from Spec-R); only EM can put an NP argument into a theta position. Thus, IM is blocked here. Suppose, then, that we build a duplicate of *the fox* and try to EM this duplicate into the subject position, yielding

(66)   WS = [{X, {v^*, {(IA), {R, IA}}}}] where X = a duplicate of {the, fox} built
         independently

EM of X into the theta Spec-of-v^* position is allowed by Preservation; it's EM of an argument to create a theta position. However, once FC(X, IA) applies at the phase level, we have a violation of TT, and specifically univocality: X=IA=*the fox* is getting more than one theta role from the same theta role assigner, namely, the v*-R complex.[80] There is thus no way to generate (63) on the intended interpretation, neither by IM nor by EM. As a final point, we are adopting the simplest assumption that FC is optional. If FC(X, IA) does not apply in (66), then we get a legitimate derivation for the well-formed 'The fox chased the fox' (where there are two foxes), the right result.

The passive (62), on the other hand, is perfectly fine. We start again with (65), and Merge in INFL (I) but since the syntactic subject of a passive construction is not a position to which a theta role is assigned, nothing prohibits IM of the IA to create the (non-theta) Spec-of-INFL position.[81] The result of such Internal Merge is:

(67)   WS = [{X, {I, {v, {(IA), {R, IA}}}}}]

Since passive v does not assign a theta role to the Spec-of-*v* position, FC(X, IA) can apply without violating univocality.[82] Thus (X, IA) are copies, the lower copy is not pronounced, and we derive the surface for *The fox was chased*. Similar reasoning holds for object raising in unaccusative sentences, subject-to-object raising (ECM), and subject-to-subject raising.

Consider, for instance, the key points of the derivation of ECM construction (68):

(68)   I expected the fox to eat crisp apples.

The lower semantic subject, *the fox*, is externally merged into the Spec-of-*v*-EAT:

(69)   WS = [{EA, {v*, Z}}]   EA = {the, fox}, Z = {EAT, {crisp, apples}}

This is EM of an argument into a theta position, sanctioned by Duality. Since the infinitival clause is the IA of *expect*, we assume there is no intermediate phase CP. We then Merge in the ECM root EXPECT.

(70)   WS = [{R, {to, {EA, {v*, Z}}}}] R = EXPECT

Now EA can internally merge into the non-theta Spec-of-R position (for Case and labeling). By Search, the lower EA inscription is inaccessible and hence the

---

[80] Note that there is an alternative explanation for why FC is blocked in (66): the PIC; that is, FC cannot apply across the phase head. Under this view (66) is disallowed since FC(X, IA) can't apply, meaning that X and IA are repetitions, yielding *The fox chased the fox* (two different foxes); but not *The fox chased* (meaning the fox chased itself). In control cases like, *Bill tried to ~~Bill~~ leave*, FC could apply on the assumption that both instances of *Bill* are within the same phase. See Chomsky (in press) for further comments.

[81] Here we make the standard distinction between weak v (not a phase head) and strong v* (is a phase head). We put aside issues with the merge of *to*.

[82] And under the alternative view suggested in footnote 80, FC could apply here since both of the identical inscriptions are included in the same phase. See Chomsky (in press) for further consequences.

WS has not expanded. Finally, we merge in the higher phase head v^* (and its external argument X):

(71)   WS = [{X, {v^*, {EA, {R, {to, {~~EA~~, {v^*, …}}}}}}}}]

Here, FC({the, fox}, {the, fox}) applies, ultimately yielding (68), after externally merging INFL and internally merging external argument X to Spec of INFL. Raising structures like (72) pattern in essentially the same way.

(72)   a. the student seems to be confused by the new concepts/happy about the
              assignment/ etc.
          b. the student was expected to be confused by the new concepts/happy about
              the assignment/ etc.

We see, then, that the various first and third-factor principles conspire to constrain the application of Merge, yielding just the right empirical results in these core cases.

6.2 The Enabling Function of SMT

Let's turn now to further details on obligatory control, which, as outlined in Section 5, follows, without any additional mechanisms, from the framework reviewed here.

Consider a typical instance of obligatory control:

(73)   The man tried to sleep.

The derivation proceeds as follows. We first build the lower, infinitival clause.

(74)   WS = [{to, {EA, SLEEP}}]   where EA = {the, man}

We assume that there is no lower CP. The matrix root TRY is introduced into the WS and externally merged with the infinitival, followed by the introduction and merger of matrix v^*:

(75)   WS = [{v^*, {TRY, {to, {EA, SLEEP}}}}]

Given Preservation, the lower external argument (EA) *{the, man}* can't be internally merged from the lower (theta position) to the Spec-v^* position, that is, to the higher external argument position: IM is only to non-theta and not to theta positions.[83] But another option is available. First, we build within the WS a duplicate instance of {the, man}, completely independent of the first:

(76)   WS = [{the, man}, {v^*, {TRY, {to, {EA, SLEEP}}}}]

---

[83] We leave open the exact status of the infinitive marker *to*. It could be argued that *to* is a morphological reflex of the bare form of the verb. In any case, whether the EA moves through Spec of *to*, the EA can't IM into the higher Spec of TRY position, given Preservation.

We now externally merge this new instance of {the, man} to Spec-v*; this is EM of an NP argument creating a theta position, sanctioned by Preservation:

(77)   WS = [{{the, man}, {v*, {TRY, {to, {EA, SLEEP}}}}}]

This matrix v*P is a phase and thus FC and labeling apply. FC will apply as FC ({the, man}, EA), rendering these structurally identical inscription copies. The lower copy, EA, is not pronounced at SM if externalization is opted for. The phase-head complement is transferred and now inaccessible for further syntactic operations, given the PIC:

(78)   WS = [{{the, man}, {v*, {TRY, {to, {EA, SLEEP}}}}}]

Crucially, the result here does *not* violate TT since {the, man} and its structurally identical copy, EA (= {the, man}), get a theta role from *different* theta role assigners, in complete conformity with univocality.

Next, we construct the higher C phase (79) in three steps, where EA$_2$ stands for {the, man} in (78):

(79)   WS = [{C, {EA$_2$, {I {EA$_2$, {v*, {TRY, {to, {EA, SLEEP}}}}}}}}]

INFL is merged into the structure. EA$_2$ is merged by IM to non-theta Spec-INFL, followed by the merger of C. At this phase level, FC applies, FC(EA$_2$, EA$_2$) assigning the copy relation to these structurally identical inscriptions of {the, man}.[84] Since they are copies, they are interpreted in the same way and, if externalization is activated, only the higher one is pronounced, yielding (73). Such a derivation is perfectly legitimate under the framework here.[85] The existence of obligatory control is thus an immediate consequence of SMT, a significant result.

A significant consequence of this analysis is that we do not lose the traditional distinction between trace and PRO, which now can be characterized as copy-of-IM versus copy-with-EM. Traditionally, PRO and NP-trace were separate objects with a distinct featural makeup. A cluster of properties distinguished the *NP-trace* relation and the *NP-PRO* relation. In our framework, 'trace' and PRO are eliminated and thus there is a conceptually attractive reduction of the

---

[84] We assume transitivity of the FC relation.

[85] We assume that FC applies optionally. The assumption leads to an empirical consequence, namely potentially SM-blocked but CI-convergent derivations of *John tried Mary/John to win*, raising factual questions that there is no obvious way of answering.

Note furthermore that FC is constrained by MS, as is attested by contrasts like,

(i)   *John was introduced John to ~~John~~
(ii)   John was introduced ~~John~~ to John

where (i) is correctly disallowed by MS.

inventory of theoretical postulates. In current terms, for all relevant cases, FC (NP, NP) applies in a c-command configuration and the 'trace' versus 'PRO' distinction simply falls out from independent principles. To illustrate, consider raising and control,

(80)   a. NP seems [NP to win]   = the man seems to the man win   = 'trace'
       b. NP tried [NP to win]   = the man tried to the man win   = 'PRO'

In each of the two structures, the relation between the NPs is the same in that they are copies resulting from FC(NP, NP) applying at the phase level. The distinction is not in the featural makeup of the elements themselves (as was the case with *trace* vs *PRO*). Looking just at the representations (80a) and (80b) themselves, as FC does, there is no distinction between the lower NPs. However, the *derivations* associated with the two are distinct and this distinction is naturally detected by the interpretive component at the point that interpretation takes place: in (80a), the lower NP was internally merged to the higher position, whereas in (80b) the lower and higher NPs were created independently and each was externally merged into its respective theta position. The lower copies in (80a) and (80b) are structurally identical elements in a theta position c-commanded by some higher structurally identical NP. The interpretive component can detect a difference by being equipped with thematic information: the lower copy functions as 'PRO' if its c-commanding identical element occupies a theta position; otherwise, it is 'trace.' When they function as trace or PRO is thus deducible.

The crucial distinction is whether the structure is created by IM (for 'trace') or by EM (for 'PRO'). We've already detailed the derivation associated with control, (80b). Let's turn then to (80a). Suppose we have built up to:

(81)   WS = [{I, {seems, {to, {NP_1, win}}}}] (Subscripts are used only for ease of exposition and NP = {the, man}.)

Crucially, at this point, we *internally merge* NP_1 and IP

(82)   Merge(NP_1, IP, WS)   where IP = {I, {seems, {to, {NP_1, win}}}}

The output of the Merge application specified in (82) is (83):

(83)   WS' = [{NP_1, IP}]

By looking over the steps of the derivation, which Preservation by definition has access to, Preservation can detect the *identity* relation between NP_1 in (81) and NP_1 in (83); it is the very same NP_1 inscription, and Preservation is satisfied since the raised NP does not accrue an additional theta role and hence does not change meaning. As we've seen, this identity relation does not hold with control; with control, separate instances of the NP are created and put into the copy relation by FC.

In this way, the classic trace versus PRO distinction arises, not by stipulation but as a natural consequence of SMT. Consider, for instance, the contrast in (84) from Burzio (1981, 1986)[86]:

(84)   (a) one interpreter each seems [t to have been assigned t to the diplomats]
         (b) *one interpreter each tried [PRO to be assigned t to the diplomats]

This distinction arises not because of a distinction between PRO and trace, but because of the difference in the derivation of the two structures: (84a) involves IM of *one interpreter* from the positions marked *t* and reconstructed in that position, while in (84b), there are two separate instances of *one interpreter* (as we have just detailed) given Preservation, and there is no reconstruction; rather, interpretation of an independent element, and thus *each* is stranded. Similar reasoning holds for the other classic cases of the traditional trace versus PRO distinction, including (85) versus (86), from Chomsky (1965),[87]

(85)   a. John persuaded the doctor [PRO to examine Bill]
         b. John persuaded Bill [PRO to be examined by the doctor]

(86)   a. John expected the doctor [t to examine Bill]
         b. John expected Bill [t to be examined by the doctor]

where (85a) and b have a distinct interpretation, while (86a) and b are interpreted in the same way. The distinction follows from structurally identical inscriptions being derived from IM, in which case in the eyes of Preservation they are in fact one and the same inscription, as opposed to the structurally identical inscriptions being constructed from separate instances of EM. What is traditionally referred to as 'trace' is the identity relation ensured by FC; while PRO is a separate instance of NP put into the copy relation via FC. As noted in Chomsky (2021b, p. 22): "The distinction between the two kinds of copy seems well established from several perspectives. It therefore provides empirical

---

[86] There are many additional illustrations of the trace versus PRO distinction. Thus Kayne (1975) gives:

i.   Jean se force t_{IA} [PRO à être fort]
ii.   *Jean se semble t_{DAT} [t_{EA} être intelligent]

See also Burzio (1986) for similar cases in Italian. These also follow from the present framework. See Chomsky (2021b) for a range of additional examples.

[87] It should be noted that the Aspects model of Chomsky (1965) did not use 'trace,' but, presupposing object raising, the contrast in (85)/(86) translates to the trace versus PRO distinction.

support for the assumption that the Duality principle . . ., on which the distinction rests, is indeed an LSC [Language Specific Condition]."

There are therefore a number of different relations between structurally identical inscriptions: Identity, Copy, Repetition. The identity relation is one that can only be detected across steps of a derivation. Thus, in the mapping from (87) to (88), via Merge(NP_1, IP, WS), the inscriptions in the input and output WS are identical, the very same inscription:

(87)   WS = [{I, {seems, {to, {NP_1, win}}}}]
         $NP_1 = NP_1$ (the identity relation)

(88)   WS' = [{NP_1, IP}]

However, relative to just the output representation itself, fully articulated as

(89)   WS' = [{NP_1, {I {seems, {to, {NP, win}}}}}]

the relation between the structurally identical inscriptions NP_1 and NP is one of copy, assuming FC(NP_1, NP) at the phase level. In effect, FC confirms the identity relation of an application of IM. But FC also applies in some cases of EM, as in control. Finally, structurally identical inscriptions can be repetitions, as in, say, *Many people praised many people* (where, as we've seen, there are distinct two sets of people). In short, *structurally identical inscriptions* can be *identical* or not. In the former case they are IM-derived (IM-trace); in the latter case they may be either copies by FC (EM-PRO) or repetitions, independently generated. The interpretive component, equipped with Duality, can see this difference relative to the representations to which it applies: the matrix subject is in a non-theta position (hence 'trace') or in a theta position (hence 'PRO').

7 On the History and Development of Merge

In this section, we trace certain aspects of the developmental history of Merge. It is not intended as a comprehensive history of minimalism, but will focus instead on issues directly related to Merge itself. We first highlight the progression from phrase structure rules to Merge in early and middle minimalism. We then consider Merge from a wider lens, noting that in one sense Merge represents the type of bottom-up approach of the earliest analyses in Generative Grammar, as opposed to the top-down approach of, say, government and binding theory.[88]

As mentioned at the outset of this Element, what we find throughout the history of the development of the generative enterprise is a reduction of the

---

[88] For similar comments on the history of Merge, see Epstein and colleagues (2022), from which this section draws.

inventory of theoretical postulates within the narrow syntax. Language- and construction-specific rules, and syntax-internal and syntax-specific principles and mechanisms have been reduced, factored down, or eliminated. The effects of these postulates were (in large part) derived from general principles of computational systems – notions of computational efficiency, for example, of 'least effort' (as we've seen), ideally laws of nature. This quest for parsimony is the norm in the sciences. As John Wheeler (1989) stated it: "Surely someday, we can believe, we will grasp the central idea of it all as so simple, so beautiful, so compelling that we will all say to each other, 'Oh, how could it have been otherwise! How could we all have been so blind so long!'" Let's trace some of the details of this reduction.

7.1 Phrase Structure Rules, from Bottom-Up to Top-Down

Recall from Section 1 the paradox of discrete infinity: a finite set of atomic elements and a finite number of computation operations can generate an infinite array of linguistic expressions, the so-called infinite use of finite means.[89]

This infinite use of finite means, now understood in the context of recursive function/Generative Grammar theory, is the core 'creative' property of human knowledge of syntax. In the context of the development of Merge, it is important to note that in the earliest stages of the theory, Chomsky (1955/1975) (the Logical Structure of Linguistic Theory [LSLT]), the recursive property resided in the 'transformational' component, more specifically in the *generalized* transformations that inserted basic (so-called kernel) structures already modified by *singulary* transformations into a new structure, which then itself underwent singulary transformations before being inserted by a generalized transformation into yet another structure, and so on (i.e., cyclic, bottom up, and derivational). Three important, related, observations on properties of LSLT that have 'corresponding' properties in Merge theory are to be noted. For one, the system employed radically bottom-up derivation with cyclic application of rules, with an understood WS for parallel generation of kernel structures before one being inserted into the other. Singulary and generalized transformations were interspersed, similar (at least in some respects) to the fact that in the current theory EM and IM are unordered with respect to one

---

[89] It should be noted, however, that this is a standard misinterpretation of Humboldt, who was talking about the 'creative use' of an internal system, that is, production ('performance'), not generation by a recursive system that made creative use possible ('competence'), a distinction that did not exist clearly until mid-twentieth century (Chomsky 1965, 1966a).

another. And finally, a representational level of Deep Structure was unformulable,[90] as is true under current theory.

Only later, in the shift to the *Aspects* framework of Chomsky (1965) was recursion located in the PS component. As we'll see directly below, Chomsky formulated a recursive base component (the structure S became a recursive element) so that generalized transformations were no longer necessary to produce clausal embedding, allowing Deep Structure and Surface Structure to be precisely defined as distinct levels of representation. Deep Structure generation was top-down, while transformations operated bottom-up. In important respects, then, a Merge-based theory is similar to LSLT.[91]

The recursive phrase structure rules developed in *Aspects* represented a valuable step in structure building. But, empirically, the system had to face the pervasive empirical phenomenon of displacement:

(90)   *Who did you visit?*

where *who* is, in effect, in two positions at once – abstractly it's:

(91)   *who did you visit who*

where *who* is interpreted relative to its position as the object of *visit,* but *who* is pronounced relative to its position as the initial element of the sentence.[92]

So, more than just PS rules were needed. A different set of operations, embedded within the *transformational component,* was proposed. These operations took the hierarchical phrase structure built by PS rules as input, manipulated it in various ways, crucially including displacement, and gave a modified phrase marker as output. Thus, it seemed during the pre-Merge period that two fundamentally different components were necessary:

(92)   phrase-structure building operations (PS rules) and

(93)   phrase-structure altering operations (transformations).

Through most of the history of the theory, displacement (one property of the transformational operations) was considered an oddity and a complication:[93]

---

[90] The terms Deep Structure and Surface Structure refer to levels of representation within the earlier framework (see in particular Chomsky 1965), where Deep Structure was an abstract representation resulting from the application of certain rules (phrase structure rules plus lexical insertion) that could then be mapped onto Surface Structure via transformational operations. The bottom-up Merge-based framework eliminates these levels of representation.

[91] The comparison of the Merge system with LSLT is necessarily imprecise as they are conceptually quite different.

[92] Its scopal properties are also determined from the clause-initial position.

[93] In fact, various alternative programs emerged, some attempting to eliminate the transformational component; see, for instance, Harman (1968); the GPSG framework of Gazdar; see

why would human linguistic systems have displacement, whereby the sound of a category is determined relative to one position, but its meaning is determined relative to another (e.g., *who* in *Who did you visit?* as discussed above), a nonoptimal design with respect to communicative efficiency. As is well known from the parsing literature, comprehension of sentences displaying displacement of a *wh*-phrase, yielding 'filler-gap'[94] dependencies, imposes a burden on the speech perception device.[95] On hearing *who* at the outset of such a sentence, the comprehender's parser must store this NP, continue parsing the ensuing input, and then identify the position from which *who* was moved, thereby recovering the meaning structure. For now, we note that at the time there was no explanation for displacement beyond the statement that transformations had defined within them the power to carry out the dissociation.[96] As we will see later, an explanation had to await the introduction of Merge; an explanation for displacement phenomena in terms of hierarchical structure was essentially unformulable with only the rewrite rules of phrase structure grammar, whose concern was the generation of terminal strings (weak generative capacity). The structure it could express was the kind of structure that could be determined from *any* derivational sequence of a generable string. This was unprincipled because any grammar that fulfilled the task would be a success. But more importantly, linguistically significant generalizations could not be expressed, and explanatory adequacy was beyond reach (Chomsky 1956). Structure dependence of rules and of displacement showed the inadequacy of string-based rewrite systems (Berwick et al. 2011; cf. Chomsky 1980). To overcome these fundamental shortcomings and attain some level of explanatory adequacy, transformational rules that map phrase markers (PMs) onto PMs were introduced to explain, rather than merely describe, the structure of displacement. The

---

Gazdar and colleagues (1985); the LFG framework of Bresnan – see, for example, Bresnan (1982); see also Steedman (1987) on CCG; and the Functionalist Grammar of Dik (1987) and later work.

[94] The so-called 'filler' refers to *who* in initial position, and the 'gap' is the object position of *visit* with respect to which *who* is interpreted. In fact, as was noted, *who* has a dual interpretation, an interpretation relative to object position (its theta role), and an interpretation relative to the operator position binding the object; that is, *who* is also interpreted as a quantifier binding a variable in VP, hence it's interpreted in the higher position as well.

[95] See Chomsky (2019b) for detailed discussion. It would seem that language is not particularly well designed for efficient communication, contra the twentieth-century behaviorist/structuralist conception that sees language as fundamentally a system of communication, still virtual dogma in philosophy of language and most of cognitive science.

[96] Nor could displacement be explained in string-producing rewriting systems. At best it could be 'described' (weak generative capacity of terminal strings). Tree structure is ruled out for string sets of mildly context-sensitive languages like Swiss German (Huybregts 1984; Schieber 1985). But also for simple context-free grammar, displacement was a problem (forcing extra devices, 'slash features' of PGSG simulating 'movement trajectories'). See also Gazdar and colleagues (1985).

transformational account for displacement was explanatory in the sense that it showed that *structure*, rather than *strings*, was crucial for syntax. It is precisely that distinction that resurfaces in current I-language (hierarchical structure) versus externalization (word order).[97]

Standard theory provided wide empirical coverage but questions regarding explanatory adequacy soon arose. Note, for example, that PS rules were completely unconstrained, as noted by Lyons (1968) and others, allowing such PS rules as

(94)   NP → AdvP Prep
          VP → Adj PP

In fact, however, no such rules were ever proposed. Rather, for the major lexical categories (noun, verb, adjective) what we find is endocentricity. So, we can ask: why does a rule like (95) have the properties it has?

(95)   VP → V NP

For instance, why is the 'mother node' on the left labeled VP (and not NP or something else entirely)? And more generally still, why is there a label at all; for note that at one level of abstraction (95) is no different than, say, X → Y Z; that is, it is a pure stipulation that VP is 'above V.' Within the earlier theory, these questions were simply not addressed; rather, PS rules were axiomatic and any single phrasal category could be rewritten as any sequence of categories and thus the existence and categorial status of mother labels were pure stipulation; that VP was above V in (95) is arbitrary. There was no answer to the question: Why these rules and not others? Such considerations led to the next stage in the development of structure-building devices, namely, X-bar theory.

7.2 X-bar Theory

X-bar theory represented a major development in the history of phrase structure, and represents an important step in the progress toward Merge. The basic idea is that at the right level of abstraction, all phrases (VP, NP, AdjP, etc.) had the same basic structure consisting of a *head* (a nucleus so to speak) and various elements associated with that head, something that can be referred to as the 'X-bar template.' The X-bar template imposed tight restrictions on what counts as 'humanly possible phrase structure representation,' while maintaining the crucial property of recursion. X-bar theory sought to eliminate PS rules, leaving

---

[97] For an accessible account of this, see Everaert and colleagues (2015). Chomsky (1956) was the first important study to show precisely that.

only the general X-bar-format (i.e., the abstract structure that all phrases share) as part of UG.[98]

Under X-bar theory, all phrases were strictly endocentric: each phrase was assumed to contain a unique *head* whose lexical category label determined the label of the phrase containing it. Thus, exocentric PS rules like (94) above are excluded, as is the PS rule for sentence in (96) along with the label S.[99]

(96)   S → NP VP

Ultimately, all such cases were ruled out under strict adherence to X-bar theory, as all structures must be 'headed.' A partial explanation for 'why these rules and not others' was thus possible.

Furthermore, massive simplification of the PS component resulted. Rather than the language-specific PS rules of, say, French or Japanese, there remained only the general phrasal template, the idea being that all phrases of all languages had the same abstract structure. Note further that this exposed the artificiality of 'constructions,' showing that they have no theoretical status but are rather like 'terrestrial mammal' in biology.[100]

Although it may not have been realized at the time, X-bar theory created the possibility of factoring out linear order: X-bar projections encoded the structural relations of the elements within but not their linear order. It was maybe the first step in dissociating linear order and hierarchical structure that led to the result that internal language exclusively relies on structure and ignores linear order,[101] which is relevant only in externalization. Standard PS rules conflated two relations, dominance and precedence. It was eventually realized that X-bar theory encodes dominance only, pushing linear order into another domain, ultimately to 'externalization,' that is, a property of phonological interpretation, not meaning. This disentangling of dominance and precedence, along with explaining their existence as subservient to the interfaces (dominance for

---

[98] Note that there is some similarity to Harris's Morpheme-to-Utterance procedures of analysis; see Harris (1952). Note furthermore that X-bar format alone cannot generate structures, so there was the implicit assumption that there must be some structure-building operation; one might argue something like 'generate alpha.' Under X-bar theory, only well-formed (according to the X-bar template) structures were allowed.

[99] It should be pointed out that in the original formulation of X-bar theory, Chomsky (1970), (96) was adopted; the endocentric analysis of clause structure was proposed years later in Chomsky (1986), where it was designated "the optimal hypothesis" (p. 3). Not only did it unify the phrase structure of lexical and nonlexical categories, but it seemed to be empirically motivated in terms of head-to-head relations (selection) which occur between C & T, T & V, and V & C.

[100] With the elimination of 'constructions,' there was also the elimination of such (rather pointless) questions as whether *John was expected to win* was a raising or a passive structure.

[101] A reviewer points out that "interestingly, though, even classic PS grammar itself created such a possibility." Thus, Chomsky (1965, pp. 124–126) discusses this point but, as the reviewer further notes, Chomsky (1965) rejected, at that point, removing linear order from PS grammar.

semantics, precedence for phonology) was an important step in the development of the Strong Minimalist Thesis, explored earlier.

The X-bar formulation essentially dissociates structure from linear order. In hindsight, this is a clear precursor to the current distinction between I-language and externalization. X-bar theory supplied pure structure, the importance of which was highlighted in many ways, including Tanya Reinhart's work on anaphora, which showed the primacy of structure (c-command) over linear precedence (Reinhart 1976, 1981, 1983). Still later, the *Principles and Parameters* framework clearly dissociated hierarchical structure from order. The transformational component was reduced to a single rule of Move-alpha that did not rely on order. Furthermore, such notions, in *Principles and Parameters* and in *Barriers*, as government, binding, bounding, control, and others, were all pure structure, showing steady progress in the direction of I-language (*Basic Property*) versus externalization.

Note that there remained a transformational component but like the PS component, it too was greatly simplified. General, abstract properties were factored out of the language- and construction-specific transformations of standard theory; general operations, like displacement, that transformations had in common, emerged, becoming part of a different conception of an I-language. Thus, general transformations like NP-movement and *wh*-movement resulted, these ultimately reduced to the single, simple operation: Affect-alpha; see the groundbreaking work of Lasnik and Saito (1984, 1992).

The initial state of the language faculty still consisted of two fundamentally distinct components, X-bar (structure building) and Move-alpha (displacement), but the system overall was massively simplified, with no remaining language- or construction-specific operations. We've traced a few of the steps in the historical development of structure-building operations. We've seen:

· The crucial role of recursion.
· The goal of having a theory of 'possible human phrase structure systems.'
· The removal of linear order and *the emergent role of the interfaces*.
· And overall, a massive simplification of syntactic devices.

We also see the apparent need for separate systems: structure building and transformations. Finally, we see the role of simplification, with steps toward explanation. Rather than the language-, and construction-specific operations of standard theory (the rules of French or the rules of Russian; or the rules of relative clause formation), what emerged are very general operations and principles, common to human language, while concomitantly deriving linguistic variation and deeper insight into the nature of the language faculty, without losing empirical coverage. With the emergence of the Principle and Parameters model, languages are the same in conforming to the X-bar template (and conforming to general principles), but different in linear order and in the value of certain parameters.[102]

We stress too that the general linguistic principles that arose (like, for instance, subjacency, ECP, binding conditions, or the head movement constraint), while not language or construction specific, were nonetheless specific to the faculty of language, something that underwent a radical change in the ensuing period of research. Overall, then, progress can be claimed.

But, as we see in the history of science generally, we're never satisfied. The unrelenting quest for explanation continued. X-bar theory, for instance, raised a new set of questions – again, following the theme of a continued quest for yet deeper explanation. Namely, why should there be projection, and why should it conform to the X-bar template?[103] Furthermore, the transformational component (now reduced to just Move-alpha, and more generally still, Affect-alpha, as in Lasnik and Saito 1992) remained a mystery: why should there be displacement? These questions were taken up in the next major stage of the development of the theory, what is referred to as the Minimalist Program.

7.3 From X-bar to the Introduction of Merge in *Bare Phrase Structure*

It might seem like a dramatic shift from the tree-structure representations of the *Principles and Parameters* framework traced here, to the set-theoretic representations introduced in *Bare Phrase Structure* (BPS), and generally adopted since. That is, from representations like (97) to those like (98).[104]

(97)
```
        VP
       / \
      V   NP
         / \
        Det N
```

(98) $\{V, \{V, \{N, \{Det, N\}\}\}\}$

But, in historical perspective, the change made perfect sense. As a reviewer points out, for instance, trees were generally used for expository or pedagogical purposes, but "all of Chomsky's formalizations . . . were set-theoretic," quoting

---

[102] Among many others, see Baker (2001), Lightfoot (1993), and Roberts (2019).

[103] In some cases rules were proposed for the basic structure of clause that did conform to X-bar; various possible heads were explored, such as Infl or T, but these seemed stipulative. Some phrases seemed to be exocentric, leading later to labeling theory; see Chomsky (2013, 2015), among others.

[104] For important discussion, see Fukui and Speas (1986).

Chomsky (1982b): "Suppose, then, that we adopt the set-theoretic approach to phrase markers (and in general, level markers) of Chomsky (1955), much refined and improved in Lasnik and Kupin (1977)."

With this in mind, consider a typical tree for VP. The state we're in by the early '90s was that V and the object NP are in a relation (both members of the object labeled 'V') but with no linear order specified. This nonlinearized 'membership of' relation is captured in set-theoretic terms in that sets inherently have no linear order: $\{a, b\} = \{b, a\}$. So, on the one hand, BPS continues to adopt a readily available notational device, viz set theory, whose properties are well understood, and appeals to this device to express what is needed in language, a primitive notion of membership in a relation.

But, BPS is also motivated by minimalist theory. As noted above, X-bar theory represented a major step in the continued quest for explanation, but was not exempt from explanatory scrutiny. The question emerged: Why should X-bar theory hold? Why do we find these particular relations (endo-centricity, head-to-complement, and spec-head), as opposed to an infinite number of alternative phrase structure systems; and is endocentricity really the norm? Stated in another way, and adhering to minimalist method (see Chomsky 2007), we can ask: how 'should' phrase structures be generated under minimalist assumptions?

The minimalist method is succinctly summarized as follows:

> Throughout the modern history of generative grammar, the problem of determining the character of [the Faculty of Language] has been approached 'from top down': How much must be attributed to UG to account for language acquisition? The Minimalist Program seeks to approach the prob-lem 'from bottom up': *How little can be attributed to UG* while still account-ing for the variety of I-languages attained, relying on third factor principles? (Chomsky 2007, p. 4)

Guided by this method, one question pursued in BPS is: What's the least we can say about human phrase structure; what's required by virtual conceptual neces-sity? Certainly, elements larger than lexical elements exist; phrases exist; there is in fact hierarchical structure. Thus, as Chomsky (1994, p. 4) notes: "One ... operation is necessary on conceptual grounds alone: an operation that forms larger units out of those already constructed, call it Merge ... "

So, Merge was introduced in BPS as the central structure-building operation of the narrow syntax, necessary on conceptual grounds alone.[105] And the basic

---

[105] If indeed X-bar theory requires some structure-building operation that generates structures for X-bar schemata to filter, then it is natural to ask:

idea was that Merge takes two syntactic objects, X, Y, and creates a new object out of them; thus Merge (X, Y) = {X, Y}, and then a label for the new object is constructed from X or Y. Thus, for BPS, Merge is defined as:

(99)   Merge(X, Y) = {Z, {X, Y}}, where λ is the label of the object

Take two objects (binary), X, Y; put X, Y into a set, {X, Y}, and then label that object with the syntactic category feature(s) of X or Y. PBS Merge, then, represents an important step in the development of the theory of language; and, as we've seen, it had profound consequences.

7.4 Maximizing Minimal Merge

Research since the introduction of Merge in BPS can be seen as working toward the twin interconnected goals of (i) maximizing the explanatory effects of Merge, while at the same time (ii) minimizing its form. This is in line with the Strong Minimalist Thesis (SMT), presented by Chomsky (1993, 1995) and elaborated by Chomsky (2000) and in subsequent work (as we've seen in previous sections), taking the computational system for human language to be a 'perfect system,' meeting the interface conditions in a way satisfying third-factor principles.[106]

7.4.1 Simplifying the Form of Merge: The Elimination of Labels

With respect to the simplification of Merge, under SMT, the combinatorial operation of the generative procedure assumes (by hypothesis) the simplest formulation in what comes to be called 'Simplest Merge,' a set formation device that takes objects X and Y, and forms {X, Y}, as in (99), repeated here

(99)   Merge (X, Y) = {Z, {X, Y}} where Z is the label.

Collins (2002) was the first within the generative tradition to propose that labels be eliminated from the representation of syntactic objects and thus that the output of Merge is {X, Y} rather than {Z, {X, Y}},[107] thus

(100)   Merge (X, Y) = {X, Y}

Is it possible to derive empirically desirable aspects of X-bar theory by elaborating what has been implicitly assumed and clarifying how the structure-building operation generates X-bar-conforming structures?

The question above makes the transition from X-bar theory to Merge a natural move.

[106] See Chomsky (2000, 2007, 2008).

[107] See also Seely (2006) and see Collins and Seely (2020).

Building on earlier ideas, e.g. Moro (1997, 2000), the absence of syntactic-ally encoded labels is exploited in important new ways in Chomsky (2013, 2015), where Merge, defined in the simplest form, also applied freely. Of course, Merge is third-factor compliant; thus it conforms to such principles as the proposed *Inclusiveness Condition*, "no new objects are added in the course of computation apart from arrangements of lexical properties" (Chomsky 1995, p. 228), and the *No-Tampering Condition* (NTC), "Merge of X and Y leaves the two SOs unchanged" (Chomsky 2008, p. 138).[108]

In adopting simplest Merge, the syntactic objects it creates (as in Chomsky's 2013 analysis, aka PoP) do not have labels (clearly not in the sense of BPS). How then is the information encoded by labels derived? The answer in PoP is:

(101)   The object-identifying information is derived via third-factor Minimal Search.

What information does PoP focus on? PoP assumes that syntactic objects must be identified, not just for interpretation at the CI and SM interfaces, but for legibility more generally; an object must be identified as verbal, nominal, and so on. Thus, PoP states:

(102)   "For a syntactic object SO to be interpreted, some information is necessary about it: what kind of object is it?" (PoP: 43)

An unidentified SO is not interpretable at the interfaces.

For PoP, object-identifying information cannot be provided by syntactically represented labels for the simple reason that there *are no such labels* (i.e., there is no 'VP' above V+NP). The identification information of the label-less syntactic object $\{X, Y\}$ must be provided only by what is already present in $\{X, Y\}$. That is, it must be provided by X and/or Y, since that's all there is. And this is precisely what PoP does. Consider a simple verb phrase. As noted above, with a classic tree-structure representation, the label *VP* is providing the infor-mation that the object, namely V+NP, is 'verbal.' Deconstructing the label, we see that, informally speaking, it has two 'parts': the 'V' and the 'P.' V provides the information 'verbal' by virtue of V bearing verbal features, but note that the V of 'VP' is just a copy of what's already part of the syntactic object, namely the verb V itself. The 'P' provides the information that it's a phrase (and not a bare verb); hence VP $\neq$ V. Consider now the simplest Merge representation adopted by PoP for the VP, namely $\{V, NP\}$. The information that it's a phrase is already (and inherently) encoded by the set brackets $\{\ldots\}$. It's a 'phrase' because it's a set (i.e., it's not a lexical item); hence the information 'phrase' follows

---

[108] Note that in the version of Merge theory proposed in Sections 3–6, NTC is a consequence of Preservation, which also explains Duality and requires that deletion follow from an economy principle of externalization.

automatically. What about the information that the set (i.e., the phrase) is 'verbal'? Somehow, we need to retrieve the relevant features (verbal vs nominal, etc.) that are inherently borne by individual lexical items. The object-identification information of phrases does not arise out of the blue; in fact, it's provided by lexical material. The 'verbal' of VP is clearly derived from the fact that its head is a verb; it's the lexical features of the verb that ultimately serve as the identifier of the larger object. With PoP's representation {V, NP}, the identifying features are located in V via the independently available, third-factor, principle of Minimal Search.

With respect to the SO {V, NP}, at the phase level, Minimal Search MS 'looks into' the set and finds its two members: V and NP. NP is itself a set and *qua set*, it has no object-identifying features, which is to say that a set has no lexical features; in fact, it has no linguistic features at all (a set is not a lexical item). The lexical item V, on the other hand, bears relevant lexical features, in this case the features 'verbal.' This featural information is automatically provided by third-factor Minimal Search, and the information is used by the interfaces to identify the object; that is, the information 'verbal' is appealed to for object identification. The search results are freely provided by Minimal Search; in the case of {V, NP}, it basically says: I found a set (=NP) and a verbal element V; that is, I found the two members of the set I'm searching. The interfaces in fact can use the information 'verbal' and do so, interpreting the object as such; the interfaces avail themselves of information that is automatically given for free by Minimal Search.

The matter gets more complicated with 'exocentric' structures such as {NP, VP}, where there is no single head found by Minimal Search. PoP provides further, natural mechanisms, ultimately appealing to Minimal Search; we put aside those additional details here; see Chomsky (2013, 2015), see also Epstein and colleagues (2016), for discussion.

Thus, PoP takes labeling to be the process of finding the relevant object-identifying information of {X,Y} generated by Merge. PoP proposes that such labeling is "just minimal search, presumably appropriating a third factor principle, as in Agree and other operations" (Chomsky 2013, p. 43). So, labeling is not syntactically represented. No new categories are created in the course of a derivation (which, in fact, reduces to Inclusiveness). 'Labeling' is simply the name given to the independently motivated Minimal Search procedure, itself third factor and hence not stipulated. PoP eliminates labels and projection, replacing it with a labeling algorithm that is an instance of the general principle of Minimal Computation, hence gaining yet greater depth of explanation.

7.4.2 Maximizing the Effects of Merge

As noted in subsection 7.3, the history of Merge since its introduction in BPS can be seen as the steady reduction of its form, leading to simplest Merge as in PoP, and at the same time the maximization of its effects, that is, the postulation of as few operations beyond Merge as possible, and thus deducing from Merge as much as possible. As Chomsky (2001, p. 3) in "Derivation by Phase" notes "While Merge 'comes free,' any other operation requires justification." A far-reaching thesis is that Merge is the *only* narrow syntax operation.[109]

There are a number of important examples of maximizing the effects of simplest Merge. For example, the only relations available to narrow syntax were those established by Merge, that is, set membership and the probe–goal relation (see Chomsky 2008 and Epstein et al. 1998 for further discussion). The government relation of GB could no longer be formulated in minimalist terms. The binding relation involved c-command and co-indexing, but indices were banned by *Inclusiveness/NTC*, and c-command became a derivative relation. C-command figured in agreement and movement; movement must be to a c-commanding position for proper binding of its trace. But given SMT, since Merge, specifically IM, operates at the root (i.e., operates on a member of the WS), the c-command relation between the copies follows as a consequence. Furthermore, Agree could be seen as an effect of Minimal Search for a probe–goal relation.

Without a concept of government on which to formulate a notion of governing category, principles formulated in terms of governing category could not be maintained. This included the PRO-theorem of control theory and the principles of binding theory on which the theorem was based, as well as case theory and the *Barriers* theory of bounding, which subsumes the Empty Category Principle (ECP) and the Constraint on Extraction Domains (CED). The elements entering into these principles were no longer formulable and had to be eliminated. However, a formidable problem arose: how do we explain the empirical effects of these former principles? After all, *Principles and Parameters* had been an incredibly rich paradigm that had addressed significant theoretical questions involving masses of interesting empirical phenomena from a wide variety of languages. That was not a question that could be immediately answered for any/some of these cases. But there were successes, some sooner than others. The bounding theory has been reformulated in phase-based generation as a Third-Factor Resource Restriction (see Chomsky 2008). The Empty Category Principle

---

[109] The strongest view is that Merge is not just the only structure-building operation, but the only operation at all, relegating Agree to externalization; see Epstein and colleagues (2022) and Chomsky and colleagues (2019) for discussion.

was unified with EPP under general labeling requirements (see Chomsky 2013). Obligatory Control has received a principled explanation under the enabling function of SMT that allowed FC to apply to cc-configurations of structurally identical inscriptions (see Chomsky 2021b and the discussion in Section 6). Binding had been already discussed in Chomsky 1993 as an element of CI interpretation, perhaps a variant of FC. Finally, Subject Island effects, accounted for by CED, should now be explained under segregation of A- and A-bar systems (see Section 8).[110]

A particularly far-reaching example of the maximization of Merge is the reduction of the transformational component to structure building, that is, the reduction of PS rules and transformations to a single operation of simplest Merge, which constructs hierarchical structures with no designated linear order or labeling.[111] We've stressed that through much of the history of Generative Grammar, PS grammar and transformational grammar (TG) were considered fundamentally distinct, consisting of the unique component-internal operations of structure building, on the one hand, and structure manipulation on the other. But, beginning with Kitahara (1995, 1997) and continuing through Chomsky (2013, 2015) and beyond, we find that PS grammar and TG can be collapsed into simplest Merge. Merge(X, Y)={X, Y} unifies modes of application: X and Y can be separate (External Merge) or one of X, Y can be contained within the other (Internal Merge), and these applications just correspond to structure building (contiguity) and displacement (discontiguity), respectively. Thus, Merge can take as input

(103)   {the, women}, {eat, apples}

target the two syntactic objects {the, women} and {eat, apples}, and form from them the new object,

(104)   {{the, women}, {eat, apples}}

But Merge can do exactly the same thing with the input in

(105)   {{the, women} {eat, {which, apples}}}

targeting the two syntactic objects {{the, women} {eat, {which, apples}}} and {which, apples} resulting in

(106)   {{which, apples}, {{the, women} {eat, {which, apples}}}}

---

[110] See Freidin and Vergnaud (2001) for important discussion. On the reduction of the control component to movement, see O'Neil (1995) and Hornstein (2001).

[111] In early minimalist proposals Merge (composition) and Move (displacement) replaced X-bar and Move-alpha, respectively. Merge was then reformulated as EM and Move as IM, and still later EM/IM were unified under simple Merge.

and this just is displacement, assuming copies.

As we noted in subsection 7.1, throughout much of the history of Generative Grammar one question was: Why is there displacement? And no particularly insightful answer could be given. But with simplest Merge, and following the Strong Minimalist Thesis, it reduces to the new (and much deeper) question: Why is there Merge? Once you have Merge, displacement follows for free; in fact, it would take a stipulation to avoid it.

Overall, we see the steady development of the form and function of Merge, having traced its roots in the earliest work in the generative tradition to classic PS rules, and from X-theory to the introduction of Merge in PBS. Throughout we see the simplification of Merge and the maximization of its effects, directly in line with the SMT and the quest for deeper explanation.

8 Prospects for the Future

Generative Grammar has uncovered a vast range of intricate phenomena whose accurate description and ultimate explanation are essential for the success of any syntactic theory. This Element has so far addressed only a sampling of the larger empirical picture, as our focus is on the fundamental elements of theory itself, and the establishment of a program of research consistent with rigid adherence to the Strong Minimalist Thesis. In this final section, we touch on a handful of the remaining empirical issues. Our goal here is not to develop formally explicit analyses of these phenomena, but rather to identify promising directions for future research, and important problems to be addressed, within the framework developed above. The emergent conclusion is that there is no shortage of questions to be explored, an encouraging sign, from our perspective.[112]

8.1 Directions Based on Previous Results

For many relevant phenomena, the literature offers coherent analyses, often descriptively successful, proposed within earlier or alternative frameworks. A central question is to what extent this prior work is compatible with the stringent adherence to the minimalist method advocated here, and, if not, what direction is suggested by the present framework. We focus on several cases of special interest, namely analyses of certain Across-The-Board and Control phenomena.

We first highlight Across-The-Board (ATB) movement, often analyzed in terms of multidominance. Take Citko's (2005) influential account of ATB

---

[112] For more detailed discussion of the balance between empirical coverage and the quest for explanation in scientific inquiry, see, among others, Epstein and Seely (2002, 2006).

extraction, according to which ATB as in (107) is derived via an operation designated as Parallel Merge.

(107)   a.   I wonder what Gretel recommended and Hansel read.
         b.   ... [$_{CP}$ what$_1$ [$_{INFLP1}$ Gretel recommended ~~what$_1$~~] and [$_{INFLP2}$ Hansel read ~~what$_1$~~]]

In Citko's analysis, both conjuncts share the same *what* (i.e., *what* is parallel merged from one conjunct to the other) and it's this unique object that is A-bar extracted. For reasons discussed in Section 4, we conclude that PM does not apply.[113] In fact, however, there is a way to derive the core properties of this structure (having the same 'copy' relations intended on the multidominant analysis), along with empirical merits,[114] with only the necessary mechanisms ('bare essentials') that SMT provides for Merge adopted here. Multiple, separately created instances of *what* are externally merged into their respective conjuncts. Then, one of the inscriptions of *what* (it doesn't matter in which conjunct) can be internally merged into the matrix Spec-C position, at which point Form Copy (FC) relates it to *both* lower inscriptions (Chomsky 2021a, 2021b; see Blümel 2014 for related ideas).

(108)   a.   [$_{CP}$ what$_1$ C [$_{INFLP1}$ Gretel [$_{vP1}$ what$_2$ ...]] and [$_{INFLP2}$ Hansel [$_{vP2}$ what$_3$ ...]]]
         b.   FC(what$_1$, what$_2$), FC(what$_1$, what$_3$) (indices used only for exposition)

Though space prohibits discussion of the empirical details, this kind of application of FC provides promising directions for the analysis of ATB extraction and related phenomena (e.g., parasitic gaps).[115]

Consider next a question that arises given the FC-based analysis of obligatory control. Hornstein (1999 et seq.), building on the work of O'Neil (1995, 1997), develops a Movement Theory of Control (MTC), where control involves movement of an NP from one to another theta position. As we've seen, the analysis proposed here is quite different: the FC-based approach posits EM-plus -FC; there is no IM for control, IM being ruled out by Preservation. One question involves control into adjuncts[116]. A major component of the MTC is Sideward Movement (subject to the same concerns as Parallel Merge, from the

---

[113] Besides the arguments we've already given, PM also requires a distinct notion of 'copy' more complex than the one adopted in this Element. For example, 'copy' could be implemented with indices as in Collins and Stabler (2016); see also Citko and Gračanin-Yuksek (2021, ch. 2); but note that such indices violate the Inclusiveness and No-Tampering conditions.

[114] For example, FC-based derivation also explains the impossibility of *covert* ATB movement, a result that Citko (2005) derives as a contradiction in linearization.

[115] Among the challenges for this approach is to explain the unique properties of Right-Node-Raising, such as cumulative agreement (see Citko 2017 for details).

[116] For recent discussion of adjuncts with the minimalist framework, see Bode (2020).

present perspective; see footnote 113), argued to apply for control into adjuncts as in (109).

(109)   a. Priya saw Taro after leaving work.
        b. [$_{vP}$ Priya saw Taro] [$_{PP}$ after Priya leaving work]
        c. [$_{INFLP}$ Priya [[$_{vP}$ Priya saw Taro] [$_{PP}$ after Priya leaving work]]]

The relevant adjuncts occur above the external argument's base position in Spec-vP but below its canonical surface position in Spec-INFL.[117] Hornstein (2003, pp. 30–31) argues that this requires Sideward Movement of the subject from the adjunct into Spec-vP, yielding (109b) as output, and allowing the derivation to proceed from there to (109c). This derivation is impossible for us since, as we've noted, Sideward Movement is disallowed (and note that this derivation violates Duality of Semantics/Preservation). The FC-based approach would, in contrast, construct the vP and the PP of (109b) independently, then raise one or the other inscription of *Priya* to Spec-INFL, and then apply FC to link the high inscription to both lower ones, much like what we suggested for (108). Note further that under our FC analysis of control, the NP-trace versus PRO distinction, which is crucial empirically, falls out; as detailed in subsection 6.2, if the antecedent of an NP is in a theta position, it's 'PRO,' otherwise it's 'trace.'[118]

8.2 Open Questions and Prospects for the Future

In this subsection, we touch on a number of questions requiring detailed exploration in the present framework. The first is the nature of successive cyclicity. Much previous work (e.g., Chomsky 2001 et seq.) assumes that successive-cyclic A-bar movement is forced by the Phase Impenetrability Condition (PIC), the phase level being the derivational point when an object

---

[117] Consider the Condition C effect in (i), showing that such PPs are below Spec-INFL, and the adjunct-stranding VP-ellipsis in (ii), showing that the PPs are above Spec-vP. See also Ernst (2002) and Truswell (2011).

    (i)   *He$_1$ went home after talking to John$_1$.
    (ii)   Priya saw John after leaving work, and Sita did Δ before leaving work.

[118] Note also that a promising approach presents itself for a variety of independent problems with control identified by Landau (2007), problems resistant to a movement-based account like that of Hornstein. For example, on Partial Control, Chomsky (2021b, pp. 23–24) suggests a procedure of *for*-phrase deletion (citing independent arguments from Epstein 1984 for *for*-phrase deletion in other contexts):

    a.   John arranged (for us) to meet at noon.
    b.   *John managed (for us) to meet at noon.

Partial Control would thus involve a structure quite different from that of exhaustive, obligatory control discussed in Section 5.3.

is opened up to interpretation by the interfaces. An important question has been to identify exactly which domains are phasal, which are not, and why. Among the most widely accepted phase domains are CP (at least in tensed clauses), vP (at least in active transitives), and, perhaps to a lesser extent, the nominal domain.[119] Much work has engaged this question (e.g., Citko 2011; Gallego 2012; Abels 2012; Van Urk 2020, among others), and, interestingly, in some cases the evidence remains inconclusive; it has proved difficult, for example, to determine whether PP and/or TP is a phase, or whether passive vP and/or nonfinite CP is.

A crucial piece in this puzzle is an explanation for why certain domains are phases in the first place (see Epstein et al. 2012 for an explanation of phasal status generally, and of the timing of phasal spell-out). As pointed out in subsection 3.3.2, the existence of phases is consonant with the overarching theme of computational efficiency (specifically Resource Restriction in the terms of this Element). Yet this does not in itself give us an explanation for why active transitive vP (for instance) should be phasal when passive vP is not (if that is indeed the case). Moreover, although Chomsky (2001) gives a number of prospective features associated with phasehood, Epstein (2015) points to many important questions that remain unresolved.

Also related to successive cyclicity is the segregation between the A- and A-bar systems. Though crucial in earlier frameworks, the A/A-bar distinction has recently been argued to be eliminable, with its core aspects being fully attributable to the featural properties of IM landing sites (Obata and Epstein 2011; Van Urk 2015; Fong 2022). This 'featural' understanding of the distinction diverges substantially from the traditional 'positional' understanding, facilitating new analyses of, for example, hyper-raising, among other things. The nature of, and ultimate explanation for, the A/A-bar distinction constitutes an important question which we leave open here.

Within the framework of this Element, these issues remain essential. Consider (110b), for instance, derived via IM from (110a).

(110)   a. $[_{C'}$ C $[_{INFLP}$ Emre$_1$ is $[_{AP}$ how likely ~~Emre~~ to win]]]

   b. $[_{CP}$ $[_{AP}$ How likely to Emre$_2$ win] C $[_{INFLP}$ Emre$_1$ is $[_{AP}$ ~~how likely Emre to win~~]]]

At first glance, this derivation seems to violate MY; not only is the syntactic object labeled CP in (110b) constructed by Merge, but now there are two accessible inscriptions *Emre*, where before there was only one. However, the

---

[119] That is, DP (Matushansky 2005; Jiménez-Fernández 2009, i.a.), or *n*P, if *n* heads the nominal domain.

problem is only apparent because (110) is already explained by the Markovian property of derivation. At the point in the derivation where Merge selects from WS the terms for constructing (110b), it has no knowledge of how these selections, C' of (110a) and AP, a term of C', were generated. Raising wh-AP to SPEC-C by IM, therefore, satisfies MY just like raising wh-AP to SPEC-C satisfies MY in deriving *(Guess) how rich John is.*[120]

There may be yet another way – consistent with Markovian property – of analyzing the derivation. The A-bar movement of AP in (110) is segregated from the A-movement which forms *Emre*$_1$. As such, the inscriptions *Emre*$_1$ and *Emre*$_2$ need not be considered simultaneously for MY, allowing legitimate generation of (110). This seems to us a plausible account of the remnant movement of (110), though the formal implementation of this idea must be left for future work (see Chomsky 2021b, p. 19, fn30; Epstein et al. 2022 for relevant discussion).

Another area that has proved difficult to model in earlier frameworks involves unbounded coordinate structures. Lasnik (2011) showed that neither phrase structure grammars nor generalized transformations on phrase markers could assign adequate structural descriptions to unbounded, unstructured sequences as in (111).

(111)   [$_{nP}$ Tristan, Jess, . . . and Carlos] went dancing.

The present approach could fare better here, given the availability of *n*-ary Form-Set: the *n*-ary operation is available as the general procedure at no cost, with binary Merge as a limiting case. Nevertheless, coordination retains problematic aspects. Coordination is also associated with numerous empirical puzzles, especially involving *respective*-predication.[121] It remains to be seen whether such issues of order-sensitive constructions can be overcome within the present approach.

To mention another relevant area, islands have posed consistent puzzles since their discovery by Ross (1967). One crucial problem has been to adequately identify which domains are properly characterized as islands. In many cases, research has revealed disparate sets of exceptions that have yet to be accounted for in a principled way. On the so-called Subject Island Effect, for instance, compare examples cited by Ross (1967, p. 249 f), Kluender (2004), and Chomsky (2008, pp. 147, 153). Analytical difficulties are compounded by the

---

[120] Crucially, we assume Merge *does* have knowledge that *Emre* and *Emre*$_1$ are formed by IM in generating INFLP, but this information is lost by the next mapping.

[121] The empirical puzzles involving *respective*-predication were first discussed in McCawley (1968).

fact that important judgments can be quite murky. Without a clear understanding of such data, competing analyses can be difficult to compare.

Even more fundamentally, the formal principles underlying island effects are unclear. Familiar mechanisms like the PIC are inadequate on their own to model islandhood; the PIC does not block extraction per se, just extraction beyond the phase edge (with extraction *through* the edge remaining possible). A challenge then is to identify plausible formal principles by which extraction *could* be constrained. Recent work suggests that island effects derive crucially from the *interaction* of the PIC with other, independent principles (e.g., Sichel 2018, among others, on the interaction of the PIC and Anti-Locality). Additionally, it has been well known since Miller and Chomsky 1963 that extra-syntactic factors (e.g., memory organization principles barring self-embedding, and other factors, Chomsky 1965, pp. 12–14) can have a significant effect in ostensibly syntactic phenomena. For islands, a range of different extra-syntactic principles could conceivably be relevant. Given islands' characteristically complex empirical profile, progress depends on identifying the precise contribution of independent syntactic and extra-syntactic mechanisms, especially where judgments are marginal.[122]

There are additional puzzles, ones surrounding ellipsis and deaccenting, anaphora and focus, grafts/amalgamation,[123] among others. Though we cannot discuss any of these issues in detail here, promising directions present themselves in many cases. Ellipsis phenomena (delineated in Merchant 2018 and elsewhere), for instance, violate I-language constraints, and share properties that must be part of performance (e.g., destressing/deletion of repeated material, parallelism conditions),[124] suggesting a crucial role for principles of externalization in these phenomena. A similar situation holds for many other topics. Given the framework of this Element and the set of core principles it provides (i.e., those that enter into SMT), the frontiers of understanding rest on explanatory maximization of core principles and their interactions with independent processes.

In addition to the topics above, there are interesting questions regarding the nature of operations other than Merge. Although this Element develops the hypothesis that Merge is the sole structure-building operation of narrow syntax, structure building is not all there is to syntactic derivations. There

---

[122] Recent years have seen an increased effort to identify the contribution of extrasyntactic factors, such as processing demands or pragmatic anomaly, in island effects (e.g., Miliorini 2019; Chaves and Putnam 2020; Culicover and Winkler 2022; Namboodiripad et al. 2022, among others). See also Heil and Ebert (2018) and Sedarous (2022) for intrasentential code-switching as a technique isolating syntactic contributions to extraction constraints.

[123] See Van Riemsdijk (1998, 2006) and Kluck (2011).

[124] See Chomsky and Lasnik (1993), Chomsky (1995, fn31), and Tancredi (1992).

are also non-structure-building processes that interpret the objects generated by Merge. The operation Agree is possibly the foremost among these; it does not generate structure on its own, but interprets the objects that Merge makes available. 'Head Movement' (or at least a subset of phenomena going under that name) may also be a post-syntactic operation, as proposed by Chomsky (2021b), in a similar vein to Matushansky (2006) and Harizanov and Gribanova (2019).

In this Element we have presented the form, function, and key points in the history, of the most fundamental syntactic operation, Merge. The framework reviewed and developed here strictly adheres to the Strong Minimalist Thesis; it includes the simplest form of Merge, and, appealing to natural third-factor considerations, provides an analysis entirely consistent with the conditions of learnability, evolvability, and universality, taking steps toward genuine explanation of the human language faculty.

References

Abels, Klaus. 2012. *Phases: An Essay on Cyclicity in Syntax*. Berlin: de Gruyter.

Baker, Mark. 2001. *The Atoms of Language: The Mind's Hidden Rules of Grammar*. New York: Basic Books.

Berwick, Robert C. and Noam Chomsky. 2016. *Why Only Us: Language and Evolution*. Cambridge, MA: MIT Press.

Berwick, Robert C., Paul Pietroski, Beracah Yankama, and Noam Chomsky. 2011. Poverty of the stimulus revisited. *Cognitive Science* 35, 1207–1242. https://onlinelibrary.wiley.com/doi/10.1111/j.1551-6709.2011.01189.x.

Blümel, Andreas. 2014. On forked chains in ATB-movement: Defending and newly implementing a traditional notion. In Martin Kohlberger, Kate Bellamy, and Eleanor Dutton (eds.), *Proceedings of ConSOLE XXII*, 19–38.

Blümel, Andreas and Anke Holler. 2022. DP, NP, or neither? Contours of an unresolved debate. *Glossa: A Journal of General Linguistics* 7: 1. https://doi.org/10.16995/glossa.8326.

Bode, Stefanie. 2020. *Casting a Minimalist Eye on Adjuncts*. New York: Routledge.

Borer, Hagit. 2003. Exo-skeletal vs. endo-skeletal explanations: Syntactic projections and the lexicon. In John Morre and Maria Polinsky (eds.), *The Nature of Explanation in Linguistic Theory*, 31–67. Stanford, CA: CSLI Publication.

Bresnan, Joan (ed.). 1982. *The Mental Representation of Grammatical Relations*. Cambridge, MA: MIT Press.

Burzio, Luigi. 1981. Intransitive verbs and Italian auxiliaries. PhD thesis. MIT.

Burzio, Luigi. 1986. *Italian Syntax*. Dordrecht: Reidel.

Chaves, Rui and Michael T. Putnam. 2020. *Unbounded Dependency Constructions: Theoretical and Experimental Perspectives*. Oxford: Oxford University Press.

Chomsky, Noam. 1955. The logical structure of linguistic theory. Ms., Harvard University, Cambridge, MA. Revised version published in part by Plenum, New York, 1975.

Chomsky, Noam. 1956. Three models for the description of language. *I. R. E. Transactions on Information Theory, IT-2, Proceedings of the Symposium on Information Theory, September*, 113–124.

Chomsky, Noam. 1959. A review of B. F. Skinner's *Verbal Behavior*. *Language* 35:1, 26–58.

Chomsky, Noam. 1964. *Current Issues in Linguistic Theory.* The Hague: Mouton & Co.

Chomsky, Noam. 1965. *Aspects of the Theory of Syntax.* Cambridge, MA: MIT Press.

Chomsky, Noam. 1966a. *Cartesian Linguistics. A Chapter in the History of Rationalist Thought.* New York: Harper & Row.

Chomsky, Noam. 1966b. *Topics in the Theory of Generative Grammar.* The Hague: Mouton.

Chomsky, Noam. 1968/2006. *Language and Mind.* Third Edition. Cambridge: Cambridge University Press.

Chomsky, Noam. 1970. Remarks on nominalization. In R. Jacobs and P. Rosenbaum (eds.), *Readings in English Transformational Grammar,* 184–221. Waltham, MA: Ginn & Co.

Chomsky, Noam. 1975. *Reflections on Language.* New York: Pantheon.

Chomsky, Noam. 1980. *Rules and Representations.* New York: Columbia University Press.

Chomsky, Noam. 1981. *Lectures on Government and Binding.* Dordrecht: Foris Publications.

Chomsky, Noam. 1982a. *Noam Chomsky on the Generative Enterprise: A Discussion with Riny Huybregts and Henk van Riemsdijk.* Dordrecht: Foris.

Chomsky, Noam. 1982b. *Some Concepts and Consequences of the Theory of Government and Binding.* Cambridge, MA: MIT Press.

Chomsky, Noam. 1986. *Barriers.* Cambridge, MA: MIT Press.

Chomsky, Noam. 1993. A minimalist program for linguistic theory. In Ken Hale and Samuel J. Keyser (eds.), *The View from Building 20: Essays in Linguistics in Honor of Sylvain Bromberger,* 1–52. Cambridge, MA: MIT Press.

Chomsky, Noam. 1994. Bare phrase structure. MIT Occasional Papers in Linguistics 5. Department of Linguistics and Philosophy, MIT. Reprinted in Gert Webelhuth (ed.), *Government and Binding Theory and the Minimalist Program,* 383–439. Malden: Blackwell.

[Bare phrase structure was also published in 1995 in: *Evolution and Revolution in Linguistic Theory: Essays in Honor of Carlos P. Otero,* Hector Campos and Paula Kempchinsky (eds.), Washington DC: Georgetown University Press, 51–109.]

Chomsky, Noam. 1995. The *Minimalist Program.* Cambridge, MA: MIT Press.

Chomsky, Noam. 2000. Minimalist inquiries: The framework. In Roger Martin, David Michaels, and Juan Uriagereka (eds.), *Step by Step: Essays on Minimalist Syntax in Honor of Howard Lasnik,* 89–155. Cambridge, MA: MIT Press.

Chomsky, Noam. 2001. Derivation by phase. In Michael Kenstowica (ed.), *Ken Hale: A Life in Language*, 1–52. Cambridge, MA: MIT Press.

Chomsky, Noam. 2004a. Beyond explanatory adequacy. In Adriana Belletti (ed.), *Structures and Beyond: The Cartography of Syntactic Structures*, 104–131. New York: Oxford University Press.

Chomsky, Noam. 2004b. *Generative Enterprise Revisited: Discussions with Riny Huybregts, Henk van Riemsdijk, Naoki Fukui and Mihoko Zushi*. Berlin: Mouton de Gruyter.

Chomsky, Noam. 2005. Three factors in language design. *Linguistic Inquiry* 36:1, 1–22.

Chomsky, Noam. 2007. Approaching UG from below. In Uli Sauerland and H.-M. Gärtner (eds.), *Interfaces + Recursion = Language?*, 1–29. Berlin: Mouton de Gruyter.

Chomsky, Noam. 2008. On phases. In Robert Freidin, Carlos Otero, and Maria Luisa Zubizarreta (eds.), *Foundational Issues in Linguistic Theory: Essays in Honor of Jean-Roger Vergnaud*, 133–166. Cambridge, MA: MIT Press.

Chomsky, Noam. 2011. Language and other cognitive systems: What is special about language? *Language Learning and Development* 7:4, 263–278.

Chomsky, Noam. 2012. Where artificial intelligence went wrong. *The Atlantic*, November 1. www.theatlantic.com/technology/archive/2012/11/noam-chomsky-on-where-artificial-intelligence-went-wrong/261637/.

Chomsky, Noam. 2013. Problems of projection. *Lingua* 130, 33–49.

Chomsky, Noam. 2015. Problems of projection: Extensions. In Elisa DiDomenico, Cornelia Hamann, and Simona Matteini (eds.), *Structures, Strategies and Beyond: Studies in Honour of Adriana Belletti*, 3–16. Amsterdam: John Benjamins.

Chomsky, Noam. 2017a. The Galilean challenge. *Inference* 3.1. https://inference-review.com/article/the-galilean-challenge.

Chomsky, Noam. 2017b. The language capacity: Architecture and evolution. *Psychonomic Bulletin & Review* 24, 200–203. https://doi.org/10.3758/s13423-016-1078-6.

Chomsky, Noam. 2019a. Some puzzling foundational issues: The reading program. *Catalan Journal of Linguistics* Special Issue, 263–285.

Chomsky, Noam. 2019b. The UCLA lectures. https://www.youtube.com/watch?v=c_BWbEjAUd0. [An edited transcript of the lecture with an introduction was posted on LingBuzz by Bob Frieden.]

Chomsky, Noam. 2020. The UCLA lectures: With an introduction by Bob Freidin. LingBuzz.

Chomsky, Noam. 2021a. Linguistics then and now: Some personal reflections. *Annual Review of Linguistics* 7, 1–11. https://doi.org/10.1146/annurev-linguistics-081720-111352.

Chomsky, Noam. 2021b. Minimalism: Where are we now, and where can we hope to go. *Gengo Kenkyu* 160, 1–41.

Chomsky, Noam. 2021c. Reflections. In Nicholas Allott, Terje Lohndal, and Georges Rey (eds.), *A Companion to Chomsky*, 582–594 Hoboken, NJ: Blackwell/Wiley.

Chomsky, Noam. 2022a. SMT and the science of language. Talk at MIT, April 1.

Chomsky, Noam. 2022b. Genuine explanation and the Strong Minimalist Thesis. Talk at MIT, April 1.

Chomsky, Noam. In press . The Miracle Creed and SMT. In Giuliano Bocci, Daniele Botteri, Claudia Manetti, and Vicenzo Moscati (eds.), *Issues in Comparative Morpho-syntax and Language Acquisition*.

Chomsky, Noam, Ángel J. Gallego, and Dennis Otto. 2019. Generative Grammar and the faculty of language: Insights, questions, and challenges. *Catalan Journal of Linguistics* Special Issue, 229–261.

Chomsky, Noam and Howard Lasnik. 1993. The theory of principles and parameters. In Joachim Jacobs, Arnim von Stechow, Wolfgang Sternefeld, and Theo Vennemann (eds.), *Syntax: An International Handbook of Contemporary Research*, vol. 1, 506–569. Berlin: Walter de Gruyter. Reprinted in Chomsky (1995).

Chomsky, Noam and Andrea Moro. 2022. *The Secrets of Words*. Cambridge, MA: MIT Press.

Citko, Barbara. 2005. On the nature of Merge: External Merge, Internal Merge, and Parallel Merge. *Linguistic Inquiry* 36:4, 475–496.

Citko, Barbara. 2011. Symmetry in syntax: Merge, move and labels. Cambridge: Cambridge University Press.

Citko, Barbara. 2017. Right node raising. In Martin Everaert and Henk van Riemsdijk (eds.), *The Wiley Blackwell Companion to Syntax*, Second Edition. https://doi.org/10.1002/9781118358733.wbsyncom020.

Citko, Barbara and Martina Gračanin-Yuksek. 2021. *Merge: Binarity in (Multidominant) Syntax*. Cambridge, MA: MIT Press.

Collins, Chris. 1997. *Local Economy*. Cambridge, MA: MIT Press.

Collins, Chris. 2017. Merge(X,Y) = {X,Y}. In Leah Bauke and Andreas Blümel (eds.), *Labels and Roots*, 47–68. Berlin: Mouton de Gruyter.

Collins, Chris. 2022. The complexity of trees, universal grammar and economy conditions. *Biolinguistics* 16, 1–13.

Collins, Chris and T. Daniel Seely. 2020. Labeling without labels. Manuscript. lingbuzz (lingbuzz/005486). [A revised version is to be included in Kleanthes

K. Grohmann and Evelina Leivada (eds.), *The Cambridge Handbook of Minimalism.*]

Collins, Chris and Edward Stabler. 2016. A formalization of minimalist syntax. *Syntax* 19:1, 43–78.

Culicover, Peter W. and Susanne Winkler. 2022. Parasitic gaps aren't parasitic, or, the case of the Uninvited Guest. *The Linguistic Review* 39:1, 1–35.

Curcio, Christine A., Kenneth. R. Sloan, Robert E. Kalina, and Anita E. Hendrickson. 1990. Human photo receptor topography. *The Journal of Comparative Neurology* 292, 497–523.

Dik, Simon C. 1978. *Functional Grammar.* North-Holland Linguistic Series 37. Amsterdam: North-Holland.

Einstein, Albert. 1954. *Ideas and Opinions.* New York: Bonanza.

Emmorey, Karen. 2002. *Language, Cognition and the Brain: Insights from Sign Language Research.* Mahwah, NJ: Erlbaum.

Epstein, Samuel D. 1984. Quantifier-PRO and the LF representation of PRO$_{ARB}$. *Linguistic Inquiry* 15:3, 449–505.

Epstein, Samuel D. 2015. On (I)nternalist-functional explanation in Minimalism. In Samuel D. Epstein, Hisatsugu Kitahara, and T. Daniel Seely (eds.), *Explorations in Maximizing Syntactic Minimization*, 71–97. London: Routledge.

Epstein, Samuel D. 2016. Why nurture is natural too. *Biolinguistics* 10, 197–201.

Epstein, Samuel D. and T. Daniel Seely 2002. *Derivation and Explanation in the Minimalist Program.* Malden, MA: Blackwell Publishing.

Epstein, Samuel D. and T. Daniel Seely 2006. *Derivations in Minimalism.* Cambridge: Cambridge University Press.

Epstein, Samuel D., Erich Groat, Ruriko Kawashima, and Hisatsugu Kitahara. 1998. *A Derivational Approach to Syntactic Relations.* Oxford: Oxford University Press.

Epstein, Samuel D., Hisatsugu Kitahara, and T. Daniel Seely. 2012. Structure building that can't be! In Mryiam Uribe-Etxebarria and Vidal Valmala (eds.), *Ways of Structure Building*, 253–270. Oxford: Oxford University Press.

Epstein, Samuel D., Hisatsugu Kitahara, and T. Daniel Seely. 2014. Labeling by minimal search: Implications for successive-cyclic A-movement and the conception of the postulate "phase." *Linguistic Inquiry* 45:3, 463–481.

Epstein, Samuel D., Hisatsugu Kitahara, and T. Daniel Seely 2015. *Explorations in Maximizing Syntactic Minimization.* London: Routledge.

Epstein, Samuel D., Hisatsugu Kitahara, and T. Daniel Seely. 2016. Phase cancellation by external pair-merge of heads. *The Linguistic Review* 33:1, 87–102.

Epstein, Samuel D., Hisatsugu Kitahara, and T. Daniel Seely 2022. *A Minimalist Theory of Simplest Merge*. New York: Routledge.

Epstein, Samuel D., Miki Obata, and T. Daniel Seely 2018. Is linguistic variation entirely linguistic? *Linguistic Analysis* 41:3–4, 481–516.

Ernst, Thomas. 2002. *The Syntax of Adjuncts*. Cambridge: Cambridge University Press.

Everaert, Martin B. H., Marinus A. C. Huybregts, Noam Chomsky, Robert C. Berwick, and Johan J. Bolhuis. 2015. Structures, not strings: Linguistics as part of the cognitive sciences. *Trends in Cognitive Sciences*, 19:12, 729–743. https://doi.org/10.1016/j.tics.2015.09.008.

Fletcher, H. and Munson, W. A. 1933. Loudness, its definition, measurement and calculation. *The Journal of the Acoustical Society of America* 5, 82–108.

Fong, Sandiway. 2021. Some third factor limits on Merge. Manuscript. Tucson, AZ: University of Arizona.

Fong, Suzana. 2022. Distinguishing between accounts of the A/A'-distinction: The view from Argentinian Spanish Clitic Doubling. *Isogloss* 8:2, 1–12. https://doi.org/10.5565/rev/isogloss.132.

Freidin, Robert. 2016. Chomsky's linguistics: Goals of the generative enterprise. *Language* 92, 671–723.

Freidin, Robert. 2021. The strong minimalist thesis. *Philosophies* 6, 97. https://doi.org/10.3390/philosophies6040097.

Freidin, Robert and Jean-Roger Vergnaud. 2001. Exquisite connections: Some remarks on the evolution of linguistic theory. *Lingua* 111:9, 639–666.

Fukui, Naoki and Margaret Speas. 1986. Specifiers and projection. In Tova Rapoport and Elizabeth Sagey (eds.), *MIT Working Papers in Linguistics: Papers in Theoretical Linguistics 8*, 128–172. Reprinted in Naoki Fukui. 2006. *Theoretical Comparative Syntax: Studies in Macroparameters*. London: Routledge.

Gallego, Ángel J. (ed.). 2012. *Phases: Developing the Framework*. Berlin: De Gruyter Mouton.

Gallego, Ángel J. 2020. Strong and weak "strict cyclicity" in phase theory. In András Bárány, Theresa Biberauer, Jamie Douglas, and Sten Vikner (eds.), *Syntactic Architecture and Its Consequences II: Between Syntax and Morphology*, 207–226. Berlin: Language Science Press. https://doi.org/10.5281/zenodo.4280647.

Gazdar, Gerald. , Ewan Klein, Geoffrey K. Pullum, and Ivan A. Sag. 1985. *Generalized Phrase Structure Grammar*. Oxford: Blackwell, and Cambridge, MA: Harvard University Press.

Hale, Ken and Samuel Jay Keyser. 2002. *Prolegomenon to a Theory of Argument Structure*. Cambridge, MA: MIT Press.

Harizanov, Boris and Vera Gribanova. 2019. Whither head movement? *Natural Language & Linguistic Theory* 37, 461–522. https://doi.org/10.1007/s11049-018-9420-5.

Harley, Heidi. 1995. Subject, events and licensing. Doctoral dissertation. Cambridge, MA: MIT.

Harman, Gilbert. 1968. Review of Chomsky (1966a). *Philosophical Review* 77, 229–35.

Harris, Zellig. 1952. *Methods in Structural Linguistics*. Chicago, IL: University of Chicago Press.

Hauser, Marc, Noam Chomsky, and W. Tecumseh Fitch. 2002. The faculty of language: What is it, who has it, and how did it evolve? *Science* 298, 1569–1579.

Hickok, Gregory, Ursula Bellugi, and Edward S. Klima. 1998. The neural organization of language: Evidence from sign language aphasia. *Trends in Cognitive Sciences* 2:4, 129–136.

Hinzen, Wolfram. 2017. Universal grammar and philosophy of mind. In Ian Roberts (ed.), *The Oxford Handbook of Universal Grammar*, 37–60. Oxford: Oxford University Press.

Heil, Jeanne and Shane Ebert. 2018. Extra-syntactic factors in the that-trace effect. In Contemporary Trends in Hispanic and Lusophone Linguistics, ed. by Jonathan E. MacDonald, p309–332. Amsterdam: John Benjamins.

Hornstein, Norbert. 1999. Movement and control. *Linguistic Inquiry* 30:1, 69–96.

Hornstein, Norbert. 2001. *Move! A Minimalist Theory of Construal*. Malden, MA: Blackwell.

Hornstein, Norbert. 2003. On control. In Randall Hendrick (ed.), *Minimalist Syntax*, 6–81. Oxford: Blackwell. https://doi.org/10.1002/9780470758342.ch1.

Huybregts, M. A. C. (Riny) 1984. The weak inadequacy of context-free phrase structure grammars. In G. de Haan, M. Trommelen, and W. Zonneveld (eds.), *Van Periferie naar Kern*, 81–99. Dordrecht: Foris.

Huybregts, M. A. C. (Riny) 2017. Phonemic clicks and the mapping asymmetry: How language emerged and speech developed. *Neuroscience & Biobehavioral Reviews* 81, Part B, 279–294.

Huybregts, M. A. C. (Riny) 2019. Infinite generation of language unreachable from a stepwise approach. *Frontiers in Psychology* 10. https://doi.org/10.3389/fpsyg.2019.00425.

Huybregts, M. A. C. (Riny), Robert Berwick, and Johan J. Bolhuis. 2016. The language within. *Science* 352:6291, 1286.

Jiménez-Fernández, Ángel. 2009. On the composite nature of subject islands: A phase-based approach. *SKY Journal of Linguistics* 22, 91–138.

Johnson, Kyle. 1991. Object positions. *Natural Language and Linguistic Theory* 9:4, 577–636.

Kayne, Richard. 1975. *French Syntax*. Cambridge, MA. MIT Press.

Kayne, Richard. 1981. Unambiguous paths. In R. May and J. Koster (eds.), *Levels of Syntactic Representation*, 143–183. Dordrecht: Foris.

Kayne, Richard. 1983. Connectedness. *Linguistic Inquiry* 14:2, 223–249.

Kayne, Richard 1984. *Connectedness and Binary Branches*. Dordrecht: Foris Publications.

Kayne, Richard 1994. *Antisymmetry of Syntax*. Cambridge, MA: MIT Press.

Ke, Hezao. 2019. The syntax, semantics and processing of agreement and binding grammatical illusions. Doctoral dissertation. Ann Arbor, MI: University of Michigan.

Ke, Hezao. 2022. Can Agree and Labeling be reduced to Minimal Search? *Linguistic Inquiry*. https://doi.org/10.1162/ling_a_00481.

Kitahara, Hisatsugu. 1995. Target alpha: Deducing strict cyclicity from derivational economy. *Linguistic Inquiry* 26:1, 47–77.

Kitahara, Hisatsugu. 1997. *Elementary Operations and Optimal Derivations*. Cambridge, MA: MIT Press.

Kitahara, Hisatsugu and Daniel T. Seely. 2021. Structure building under MERGE. Poster presented at WCCFL 39. [A revised version, entitled "Merge and the Formal Recognition of the Workspace" is to be included in Kleanthes K. Grohmann and Evelina Leivada (eds.), *The Cambridge Handbook of Minimalism.*]

Kitahara, Hisatsugu and Daniel T. Seely. In press. Merge and the formal recognition of the Workspace. In Kleanthes K. Grohmann and Evelina Leivada (eds.), *The Cambridge Handbook of Minimalism*.

Kitcher, Philip. 1973. Fluxions, limits, and infinite littleness: A study of Newton's presentation of the calculus. *Isis* 64, 33–49.

Klima, Edward S., Gregory Hickok, and Ursula Bellugi. 2002. Sign language in the brain: How does the human brain process language? New studies of deaf signers hint at an answer. *Scientific American*.

Kluck, Marlies. 2011. Sentence amalgamation. Doctoral dissertation. Groningen: University of Groningen.

Kluender, Robert. 2004. Are subject islands subject to a processing account? In Vineeta Chand, Ann Kelleher, Angelo J. Rodríguez, and Benjamin Schmeiser (eds.), *WCCFL 23: Proceedings of the 23rd West Coast Conference on Formal Linguistics*, 475–499. Somerville, MA: Cascadilla Press.

Koizumi, Masatoshi. 1993. Object agreement phrases and the split VP hypothesis. In Jonathan D. Bobaljik and Colin Phillips (eds.), *Papers on Case and Agreement I: MIT Working Papers in Linguistics 18*, 99–148. Cambridge, MA: MIT.

Koizumi, Masatoshi. 1995. Phrase structure in minimalist syntax. Doctoral dissertation. Cambridge, MA: MIT.

Kratzer, Angelika. 1996. Serving the external argument from its verb. In Johan Rooryck and Laurie Zaring (eds.), *Phrase Structure and the Lexicon*. Studies in Natural Language and Linguistic Theory, vol. 33, 109–137. Dordrecht: Springer. https://doi.org/10.1007/978-94-015-8617-7_5.

Landau, Idan. 2007. Movement-resistant aspects of control. In William D. Davies and Stanley Dubinsky (eds.), *New Horizons in the Analysis of Control and Raising*, 293–325. Dordrecht: Springer.

Landau, Idan. 2013. *Control in Generative Grammar: A Research Companion*. Cambridge: Cambridge University Press.

Lasnik, Howard. 2002. Clause-mate conditions revisited. *Glot International* 6:4, 94–96.

Lasnik, Howard. 2011. What kind of computing device is the human language faculty? In Anna Maria and Cedric Boeckx (eds.), *The Biolinguistic Enterprise: New Perspectives on the Evolution and Nature of the Human Language Faculty*, 354–365. Oxford: Oxford University Press.

Lasnik, Howard. 2022. On optionality: A brief history and a case study. Talk at First Biolinguistic Conference of the Université du Québec à Trois-Rivières, June 24–26.

Lasnik, Howard and Joseph J. Kupin. 1977. A restrictive theory of transformational grammar. *Theoretical Linguistics* 4, 173–196.

Lasnik, Howard and Mamoru Saito. 1984. On the nature of proper government. *Linguistic Inquiry* 15, 235–289.

Lasnik, Howard and Mamoru Saito. 1991. On the subject of infinitives. In Lise M. Dobrin, Lynn Nichols, and Rosa M. Rodriguez (eds.), *Papers from the 27th Regional Meeting of the Chicago Linguistic Society, Part 1: The General Session*, 324–343. Chicago, IL: Chicago Linguistic Society, University of Chicago.

Lasnik, Howard and Mamoru Saito. 1992. *Move Alpha: Conditions on Its Application and Output*. Cambridge, MA: MIT Press.

Lebeaux, David. 1988. *Language Acquisition and the Form of the Grammar*. Doctoral dissertation. Amherst, MA: University of Massachusetts, Amherst.

Lenneberg, Eric. 1967. *Biological Foundations of Language*. New York: John Wiley.

Lightfoot, David. 1993. *How to Set Parameters*. Cambridge, MA: The MIT Press.

Lillo-Martin, Diane C. 1991. *Universal Grammar and American Sign Language: Setting the Null Argument Parameters*. Dordrecht: Springer.

Lohndal, Terje. 2014. *Phrase Structure and Argument Structure: A Case-Study of the Syntax–Semantics Interface*. Oxford: Oxford University Press.

Lyons, John. 1968. *Introduction to Theoretical Linguistics*. Cambridge: Cambridge University Press.

Marcolli, Matilde, Noam Chomsky, and Robert C. Berwick. In press. Mathematical structure of syntactic Merge.

Matushansky, Ora. 2005. Going through a phase. In Martha McGinnis and Norvin Richards (eds.), *MIT Working Papers in Linguistics 49: Perspectives on Phases*, 157–181. Cambridge, MA: MIT.

Matushansky, Ora. 2006. Head movement in linguistic theory. *Linguistic Inquiry* 37:1, 69–109.

McCawley, James. 1968. The role of semantics in grammar. In Emmon Bach and Robert Harms (eds.), *Universals in Linguistic Theory*, 125–170. New York: Holt, Rinehart, and Winston.

Mehler, Jacques and Emmanuel Dupoux. 1994. What infants know: The new cognitive science of early development. Translated by Patsy Southgate. Cambridge, MA: Blackwell.

Merchant, Jason. 2018. Ellipsis: A survey of analytical approaches. In Jeroen van Craenenbroeck and Tanja Temmerman (eds.), *The Oxford Handbook of Ellipsis*, 19–45. Oxford: Oxford University Press.

Miliorini, Rafaela. 2019. Extraction from weak islands: Alternatives to the argument/adjunct distinction. *Revista Virtual de Estudos da Linguagem, edição especial* 17:16, 37–58.

Miller, George and Noam Chomsky. 1963. Finitary models of language users. In Robert D. Luce, Robert Bush, and Eugene Galanter (eds.), *Handbook of Mathematical Psychology II*, 419–491. New York: Wiley and Sons.

Moro, Andrea. 1997. Dynamic Antisymmetry: Movement as a Symmetry-breaking Phenomenon. Studia Linguistica 51(1), pp. 50–76. Blackwell Publishers. Oxford, UK and Malden, MA.

Moro, Andrea. 2000. Dynamic Antisymmetry, Linguistic Inquiry Monographs, MIT Press, Cambridge.

Moro, Andrea. 2016. *Impossible Languages*. Cambridge, MA: MIT Press.

Müller, Gereon. 1998. *Incomplete Category Fronting*. Dordrecht: Kluwer.

Namboodiripad, Savithry, Nicole Cuneo, Matthew A. Kramer, et al. 2022. Backgroundedness predicts island status of non-finite adjuncts in English. In *Proceedings of the Annual Meeting of the Cognitive Science Society, 44*. https://escholarship.org/uc/item/236280w2.

Nash, Neonard K. 1963. *The Nature of the Natural Sciences*. Boston. MA: Little, Brown.

Nunes, Jairo. 2001. Sideward movement. *Linguistic Inquiry* 31:2, 303–344.

Nunes, Jairo. 2004. *Linearization of Chains and Sideward Movement*. Cambridge, MA: MIT Press.

O'Neil, John. 1995. Out of control. *North East Linguistics Society* 25, Article 25. https://scholarworks.umass.edu/nels/vol25/iss1/25.

O'Neil, John. 1997. Means of control: Deriving the properties of PRO in the minimalist program. Doctoral dissertation. Cambridge, MA: Harvard University.

Obata, Miki. 2010. Root, Successive-Cyclic and Feature-Splitting Internal Merge: Implications for Feature-Inheritance and Transfer. Doctoral dissertation. Ann Arbor, MI: University of Michigan, Ann Arbor.

.Obata, Miki and Samuel David Epstein. 2011. Feature-Splitting Internal Merge: Improper movement, intervention, and the A/A' distinction. *Syntax* 14:2, 122–147.

Petitto, Laura Anne. 1987. On the autonomy of language and gesture: Evidence from the acquisition of personal pronouns in American Sign Language. *Cognition* 27:1, 1–52.

.Petitto, Laura Anne. 2005. How the brain begets language. In James McGilvray (ed.), *The Chomsky Reader*, 85–101. Cambridge: Cambridge University Press.

Ragsdale, Aaron, Timothy D. Weaver, Elizabeth G. Atkinson, et al. 2023. A weakly structured stem for human origins in Africa. *Nature* 617, 755–763. https://doi.org/10.1038/s41586-023-06055-y.

.Reed, Lisa A. 2014. *Strengthening the PRO Hypothesis*. Berlin: De Gruyter Mouton.

Reinhart, Tanya. 1976. The syntactic domain of anaphora. Doctoral dissertation. Cambridge, MA: MIT.

Reinhart, Tanya. 1981. Definite NP anaphora and c-command domains. *Linguistic Inquiry* 12:4, 605–635.

.Reinhart, Tanya. 1983. *Anaphora and Semantic Interpretation*. London: Croom Helm.

van Riemsdijk, Henk. 1998. Trees and scions: Science and trees. In Fest-Web-Page for Noam Chomsky. Cambridge, MA: MIT Press.

van Riemsdijk, Henk. 2006. Grafts follow from merge. In Mara Frascarelli (ed.), *Phases of Interpretation*, 17–44. Berlin: De Gruyter Mouton.

Roberts, Ian. 2019. *Parameter Hierarchies and Universal Grammar*. Oxford: Oxford University Press.

Rosenbaum, Peter S. 1967. *The Grammar of English Predicate Complement Constructions*. Cambridge, MA: MIT Press.

Ross, John R. 1967. Constraints on variables in syntax. Doctoral dissertation. Cambridge, MA: MIT.

Sandler, Wendy and Diane C. Lillo-Martin. 2006. *Sign Language and Linguistic Universals*. Cambridge: Cambridge University Press.

Sedarous, Yourdanis. 2022. An experimental study on the syntax of English and Egyptian Arabic: A unified account of bilingual grammatical knowledge. Doctoral dissertation. Ann Arbor, MI: University of Michigan.

Seely, Daniel T. 2006. Merge, derivational c-command, and subcategorization in a label-free syntax. In Cedric Boeckx (ed.), *Minimalist Essays*, 182–217. Amsterdam: John Benjamins.

Shi, Rushen, Camille Legrand, and Anna Brandenberger. 2020. Toddlers track hierarchical structure dependence. *Language Acquisition* 27:4, 397–409.

Shieber, Stuart M. 1985. Evidence against the context-freeness of natural language. *Linguistics and Philosophy* 8: 333–343.

Sichel, Ivy. 2018. Anatomy of a counterexample: Extraction from relative clauses. *Linguistic Inquiry* 49:2, 335–378.

Steedman, Mark. 1987. Combinatory grammars and parasitic gaps. *Natural Language and Linguistic Theory* 5, 403–439.

Tancredi, Christopher. 1992. Deletion, deaccenting, and presupposition. Doctoral dissertation. Cambridge, MA: MIT.

Testa-Silva, Guilherme, Matthijs B. Verhoog, Daniele Linaro, et al. 2014. High bandwidth synaptic communication and frequency tracking in human neocortex. *PLOS Biology* 12: 11.

Thompson, D'Arcy W. 1917. *On Growth and Form*. Cambridge: Cambridge University Press.

Tinsley, J. N., M. U. Molodstov, R. Prevedel, D., et al. 2016. Direct detection of a single photon by humans. *Nature Communications* 7: 12172.

Truswell, Robert. 2011. *Events, Phrases, and Questions*. Oxford: Oxford University Press.

Turing, Alan. 1952. The chemical basis of morphogenesis. *Philosophical Transactions of the Royal Society of London. Series B, Biological Sciences* 237: 641, 37–72.

van Urk, Coppe. 2015. A uniform syntax for phrasal movement: A case study of Dinka Bor. Doctoral dissertation. Cambridge, MA: MIT.

van Urk, Coppe. 2020. Successive cyclicity and the syntax of long-distance dependencies. *Annual Review of Linguistics* 6, 111–130. https://doi.org/10.1146/annurev-linguistics-011718-012318.

de Vries, Mark. 2009. On multidominance and linearization. *Biolinguistics* 4:3, 344–403.

Wackermannová, Marie, Ludvik Pinc, & L. Jebavý. 2016. Olfactory sensitivity in mammalian species. *Physiological Research* 65, 369–390.

Williams, Edwin. 1994. *Representation Theory*. Cambridge, MA: MIT Press.

Wheeler, J. A. 1989. "Information, Physics, Quantum: The search for links." Proceedings of the 3rd International Symposium, Foundations of Quantum Mechanics, Tokyo: 354–368. https://philpapers.org/archive/WHEIPQ.pdf

Yang, Charles. 2002. *Knowledge and Learning in Natural Language*. Oxford: Oxford University Press.

Yang, Charles. 2004. Universal Grammar, statistics or both? *Trends in Cognitive Sciences* 8:10, 451–456.

Acknowledgments

This Element reviews and elaborates a series of recent lectures and articles of Noam Chomsky, along with extended, regular, joint discussions by all the authors listed. Daniel Seely was the primary organizer and writer of the project. We thank Robert Freidin, the series editor for *Elements in Generative Syntax*, for extensive written comments, questions, and suggestions about all aspects of this Element (including the overall organization), many of which helped us bring certain key ideas and issues into sharper focus. We thank two anonymous reviewers for helpful comments and suggestions. Finally, we acknowledge our indebtedness to earlier discussion and the lasting influence of our late friend and colleague, Samuel David Epstein.

Cambridge Elements ≡

Generative Syntax

Robert Freidin

Princeton University

Robert Freidin is Emeritus Professor of Linguistics at Princeton University. His research on syntactic theory has focused on cyclicity, case and binding, with special emphasis on the evolution of the theory from its mid-twentieth century origins and the conceptual shifts that have occurred. He is the author of *Adventures in English Syntax* (Cambridge 2020), *Syntax: Basic Concepts and Applications* (Cambridge 2012), and *Generative Grammar: Theory and its History* (Routledge 2007). He is co-editor with Howard Lasnik of *Syntax: Critical Assessments* (6 volumes) (Routledge 2006).

About the Series

Cambridge Elements in Generative Syntax presents what has been learned about natural language syntax over the past sixty-five years. It focuses on the underlying principles and processes that determine the structure of human language, including where this research may be heading in the future and what outstanding questions remain to be answered.

Cambridge Elements ≡

Generative Syntax

Printed in the United States
by Baker & Taylor Publisher Services